HOW TO ATTRACT ASIAN WOMEN

What People Are Saying About This Book:

"Finally! A 'How To' book written for real people. The most complete collection of advice on dating Asian women out there. By explaining differences in cultures, Ming teaches men how to start a relationship with an Asian woman and how to carry on this relationship. She points out the 'Dos' and 'DON'Ts', teaches Asian culture, and recommends great books on Asian cultures and other topics. This book is written by an Asian woman based on extensive research of Asian women. It's the real deal, guys!" Todd, D.C.

"I love it! This book really showed me what I was doing wrong in approaching Asian women." David, MI.

"The quotes in this book by Asian women are so true!" Mike, NY.

HOW TO ATTRACT ASIAN WOMEN

Ming Tan

www.AttractAsianWomen.com
www.AsianSocials.com

BridgeGap Books
New York, New York

How to Attract Asian Women
By Ming Tan
www.AttractAsianWomen.com
Ming@AttractAsianWomen.com
www.AsianSocials.com
Info@AsianSocials.com

BridgeGap Books
New York, New York
U.S.A.

All rights reserved. No part of this book may be reproduced or transmitted in any form or by any means electronic, mechanical, including photocopying, recording or by any information storage and retrieval system, without written permission by the author.

Copyright © 2001, 2002

No copyright claimed on governmental statistics.

ISBN 0-9715808-0-4
Library of Congress Control Number: 2002102310

Cover photo courtesy of Corbis Images
Cover and interior design by Bookcovers.com

For L.T.

About the Author

Ming Tan, a Chinese-American professional who grew up in New York City, felt the need to write this book after lots of men tried to pick her up with what she felt were the wrong lines targeting her Asian ethnicity. She asked hundreds of other Asian females if men had approached them the same way, and it turned out that most of them had. Ming decided that she would write this book to help men understand and attract Asian women.

Ming founded www.AttractAsianWomen.com, a Website to help men understand and attract Asian women, and www.AsianSocials.com, the Asian American Professionals Network. To be included in the database of professionals interested in networking, please fill out an application at AsianSocials.com. You may also view personals ads posted by and chat with AsianSocials.com members by visiting AsianSocials.com. For more information, contact Info@AsianSocials.com.

When not working on helping people get together, Ming enjoys working out at the gym, museums, music, movies, fine dining and conversations with interesting people. Writing about dating and relationships is her passion.

Acknowledgments

Thanks to all the readers of www.AttractAsianWomen.com, who have encouraged me to build my Website into a great resource for helping people meet friends.

I am grateful to all the Asian ladies who patiently answered my long list of questions.

Special thanks to Brian, Marc, Terry, Let, Steve, Keith, Mary, Jen, Ann, L.T. and everyone else who has given me suggestions on this book.

Warning-Disclaimer

Most of the quotes in this chapter are candid responses from Asian female interviewees to the author's questions and do not necessarily reflect the views of the author. Also, the author does not claim to speak for all Asian women. Note that all names and identifying information of the interviewees were changed to protect their privacy.

The author, publisher, and their affiliates disclaim any and all liability resulting from the information provided in this book.

INTRODUCTION

Pssst! Ever wished you could be a fly on the wall and listen to what Asian women are saying to each other about dating, relationships and men? Now you can- just read this book! This book includes lots of quotes from Asian females who I have interviewed about dating, relationships, and men. Note that because these ladies were so candid and truthful with their opinions, some of what they said may offend certain individuals. All the quotes in italics are strictly the opinions of other Asian women and do not necessarily reflect my own views. Also, I do not claim to speak for all Asian women.

These Asian ladies ranged in age from 19 to 58; most of them live in major cities in the United States. These ladies gave candid and honest opinions on the condition that their identities not be revealed. Therefore, names and other identifying information of the interviewees have been changed to protect their privacy. However, trust that the quotes are from the ladies you would like to date. If you want to attract Asian women, listen to them! This is a must-read for any man who would like to understand Asian women. I am going to show you step-by-step how to approach an Asian woman, get her to go out with you, and how to impress her.

Asian females often get hit on by guys, both in real life and on the Internet. Sometimes, some men's approaches need a little help. Men say that beautiful Asian women can be intimidating. Often, men do not know how to act around Asian women. Have you wondered how you can get that special Asian woman to go out with you? Well, wonder no more! This guide will help you understand the minds of Asian women and win their hearts. You can use this guide to help you in relationships with Asian women all over the world; it discusses differences between the various Asian cultures. This guide applies to many Asian women, whether they have been assimilated into Western culture or have traditional Asian values, or fall somewhere in between. Again, note that the author does not claim to speak for all Asian women, and there will be exceptions to the opinions of the author and her interviewees.

How Attract Asian Women was written after years of research and personal dating experience.

One thing you should keep in mind is that you must be brave, be brave, be brave! You will never get the girl if you don't try. With the advice in this book, you will be way ahead of your competition.

TABLE OF CONTENTS

PART 1
THE PREFERENCE FOR ASIAN WOMEN

Chapter 1
Are Asian Women Different from Non-Asian Women?
— 3 —

Chapter 2
Why Men Prefer Asian Women
— 19 —

Chapter 3
Should You Put Her on a Pedestal?
— 25 —

Chapter 4
What Asian Women Think of Guys with the "Asian Fetish"
— 31 —

Chapter 5
Do Asian Women Find Non-Asian Men Attractive and Do They Want to Date Them?
— 43 —

Chapter 6
Just for Asian Men
— 57 —

Part 2
Asian Culture

Chapter 7
About Asians
— 63 —

Chapter 8
The Various Asian Cultures
— 69 —

Part 3
How to Attract Asian Women

Chapter 9
How to Enchant and Flatter that Special Asian Woman
— 103 —

Chapter 10
How to Meet Asian Women on the Internet
— 121 —

Chapter 11
How to Approach an Asian Lady
— 129 —

Chapter 12
Eleven Things You Should Never Say to an Asian Lady
— 139 —

Chapter 13
How to Act on a First Date with an Asian Woman
— 143 —

Chapter 14
What to Do to Get an Asian Woman to
Go Out with You Again
— 149 —

Chapter 15
What Makes a Man Sexy?
— 153 —

PART 1

THE PREFERENCE FOR ASIAN WOMEN

CHAPTER 1

ARE ASIAN WOMEN DIFFERENT FROM NON-ASIAN WOMEN?

Depending on how long they have lived outside of Asia, some Asian woman are definitely different from other women you might date. Asian women who grew up in Asia tend to have more traditional values when it comes to love and marriage. Asian women who are Americanized have less traditional views about love and marriage, but their Asian backgrounds still influence them. As an Asian woman who has lived in the United States for over two decades, I know myself to be different from other women; my parents instilled traditions and attitudes in me that account for the difference.

THE ASIAN EYELID FOLD

The Asian eyelid fold issue concerns women who are Chinese, Japanese and Korean, but not Filipinas and Thai women. Chinese, Japanese and Korean women often do not have a visible fold in their eyelids, and their eyes look distinctively Asian. The monolid is the most Asian of all facial features, and it distinguishes Asians from other people. Approximately 50% of Asians (and 75% of Koreans) were not born with obvious folds in their eyes. According to "Roundabout Looks" by Todd S. Inoue, in Korea double eyelid surgery is as popular as orthodontic braces in the U.S. and as many as 40% of women in Korea undergo this surgery. Korean women even pool their money together and wait for their turns to get the surgery (this Korean practice of pooling money and taking turns with the pot is called "*gye*" in Korean). Many Asian parents believe that the bigger, more Caucasian-looking eye is more beautiful, and so pressure their kids into getting plastic surgery (blepharoplasty) to alter the shape of their eyes. The American Association of Cosmetic Surgery stated that the number of eyelid operations increased from 82,520 in 1990 to 423,719 in 1999, with Asians making up the majority of eyelid surgery patients. Browse the Internet message boards frequented by Asian women, and you will see questions and tips on how to make a crease in Asian eyes. Techniques include powdering the eye and then drawing an artificial line with an eyeliner pencil, using glue and a fork to hike up the eyelid, and getting plastic surgery. One lady advised: "Go to Taiwan- it's cheaper there." Done properly, the surgery makes the eyes bigger, but still Asian looking. However, I have seen botched eye jobs that look like scars on the eyelids and look totally fake and pretentious. Do Asian women get the double eyelid surgery to look more Caucasian, or to look prettier? And what is the definition of pretty anyway? Some Asian women who want the eye surgery claim that they want it so their eyelashes do not stick down and so they can wear fake eyelashes. If the only reason for getting the eye job were for eyelashes that do not stick downwards, wouldn't it be easier getting $3.99 eyelash curler from the drugstore? I remember my mother and sister discussing whether some other women are beautiful, and the ones they found ugly always were described as having small, slanted eyes. Many Asian women get the surgery after pressure from family members to get the double eyelid surgery for bigger eyes.

The Asian standard of beauty seems to differ from the American standard of Asian beauty. In Asian cultures, the bigger and rounder your eyes, the more beautiful you are. This is the reason why the most successful models in Asia are always either half-Asian or 100% Caucasian. In the part of American society that accepts the Asian look, the single-fold Asian eye is often celebrated and called beautiful. However, many Asians are teased by their peers for looking different. What Asian child has not had their classmates stick their fingers up in the corners of their eyes to mimic the Asian look?

If you are an Asian woman considering the eyelid surgery or know someone who is, please consider the following from a Caucasian guy:

> *"Thank you so much for asking this question. Right off the bat, I have to respond with a question. Why the fascination with wanting to look 'Caucasian'??? Please don't do it ladies!!! One of the main things that makes East Asian ladies so attractive to me is precisely because they are different. I grew up surrounded by Caucasian females all my life, with the 'ideal beauty' always being the fair-skinned, blue-eyed blonde. Sure there are plenty of attractive Caucasian ladies, but I'm sorry, I just got bored with this white ideal. I needed something more, something different. Now, not that I am 100 percent up-to-date on my world demographics, but I know that there are plenty of different 'looks' out there and I doubt that this blonde blue-eyed ideal is even the majority 'look' in this world. Ladies of the world: please do not think that you have to undergo surgery, cutting up your face, to alter the way that you look so that you appear more white! Ugh!! Beauty comes in many different ways and what we need to do is celebrate the differences! You are beautiful! As I said, one of the main things that attracts me to East Asian ladies is precisely the fact that they look different from what I am used to. Add to that the fact that they are from a different culture (here I am referring specifically to East-Asian ladies that have grown up in East-Asia...not that I would turn away an Amer-Asian lady!), which makes them that much more interesting to talk with and get to know and love. It adds a whole different dimension to the lady, and adds to her depth and charm. Then, put into that already wonderful mix a warm, caring heart, and, my goodness...what more could a man ask for???*
>
> *Maybe I am making it harder on myself, striving to find what I feel in my heart, what I see in my dreams*

as my ideal lady, with plenty of eligible white ladies around me and many a sweetheart amongst their ranks. Sure, I would not have to deal with cultural differences or short-term language barriers if I stayed within my race. But why should I settle for less than what my heart is asking for? I am trying to meet up with the lady of my life, not just a plaything, a one-night stand or ease-of-getting-to-know-my-lady. I would rather be alone than settle for less than what my heart and soul are telling me that I need, and they are telling me that I need a loving, Asian lady to be my princess." Dan, MI.

One Asian woman's experience with the Asian eyelid fold:

"When I was growing up, my mother used to tell me my sister was better-looking than me because she had a bigger eye fold and bigger eyes. My mother would encourage me to push my eyelids up with my fingers until my eyes hurt to raise my eyelids a bit and to get my single-fold eyelids to crease a little. I did this everyday for a year when I was around 12 years old and eventually, I did develop a little bit of a fold. My mother was so proud of me for this. Now I was pretty in her eyes." Lilly, age 30, N.Y.

However, not every Asian woman finds her single-fold eyelids unattractive. In fact, many Asian women are proud of this distinctive Asian characteristic. Furthermore, many Asian women use eyeliner to make their eyes even more slanted, showing the world how beautiful they are. Also, not every Asian has single fold eyelids.

I caution against commenting about an Asian woman's eyelids to her, particularly upon first meeting her. At the most recent Asian dating event I hosted, an Asian lady told me that an Asian guy once gave her this dubious compliment which offended her: "Your eye folds are so deep and nice, did you get them surgically altered?" So you see, dear readers, it is not only non-Asian men who can make racially insensitive comments to Asian women. It is not only non-Asian men and Asian women who are beholden to a certain standard of Asian beauty, but also Asian men who can have different standards of Asian beauty. That is, Asian men too, can be fooled into thinking this particular kind of beauty is the only true beauty, e.g. all girls must have double eyelid folds, just as Asian women are fooled into thinking similar things.

The eyelid surgery matter raises other issues. I once spoke to a Chinese lady who called me to inquire more about my Asiansocials.com parties in New York City. I had placed an ad in a Chinese newspaper (keep in mind, when reading the following, that many Chinese Americans who can read and speak Chinese are often recent immigrants and/or people who came to the United States as adults, as was the case for this particular caller). I told her that my name is Ming and she said to me, "Why don't you have an American name?" From my conversation with the lady who asked me why I didn't have an American name, and from conversations with other Chinese ladies I spoke to who seemed eager to be assimilated into American society, it seemed that they are not just seeking non-Asian boyfriends, but an American way of life. Perhaps, then, to Asian women who prefer white or other non-Asian men, there is nothing wrong with Asian men: these women prefer non-Asian men, rather, because they perceive that Asian men cannot provide the degree of assimilation into American society that marrying an "American" will provide. Note that I am NOT saying that ALL Asian women feel this way. As one lady said: "Maybe we just fall in love because we are attracted to each other."

Quote from an Asian female:

> *"I have dated mostly white men- I guess we date who we are most comfortable with. I grew up in a white neighborhood and had little contact with Asians. Also, the Asian guys I meet don't seem to be interested in me. I have met many non-Asian men who exclusively date Asian women. Sometimes, they make me feel uncomfortable. However, I have dated mostly white*

men. Perhaps people just date who they want because they are attracted to them." Amy, NJ.

ASIAN AMERICAN IMMIGRATION

America has not always embraced Asian immigrants with open arms. Throughout American history, the United States has enacted laws that limited the number of Asian immigrants. In 1882, the Chinese Exclusion Act was enacted to stop further Chinese immigration. In 1902, the Chinese Exclusion Act was extended for another 10 years, and in 1904, Chinese exclusion was made indefinite. It was not until 1943 that the Chinese Exclusion Act was repealed. Anti-Japanese sentiment and actions during World War II further discouraged Asian immigration into the U.S. The Immigration Act of 1965 ended the discrimination of immigrants based on national origin. Instead, the act gave preference to family reunification. This act was not in full effect until the early 1970s. (It takes several years to become a naturalized citizen. Keep in mind that the laws give preference to families of American citizens.) Thus, the Asian-American population began to explode in the 1980s and 1990s, as more and more Asian-American citizens sponsored their family members in order for them to enter the U.S.

THE U.S. CENSUS

According to the most current census, there are around 5 million Asian women in the United States; 2,748,000 of these women arrived in and after 1980. 1,516,000 Asian women came to the U.S. after 1990. Between 1980-1989, 1,232,000 women born in Asia entered the U.S. Around 30% of Asian women in the U.S. arrived after 1990.

Approximately 55% of Asian women in the U.S. arrived in or after 1980. About 14% of Asian women arrived in the U.S. between 1970 and 1979. About 5% of Asian women arrived prior to 1970. This means that approximately 75% of Asian women currently in the U.S. were not born in the U.S. Furthermore, according to the

1996 Housing & Vacancy Survey, 96% of Asian-Americans are immigrants or children of immigrants.

What does mean to someone who would like to date an Asian woman in the U.S.?

There is a high probability that the Asian woman a man meets will be an immigrant. This supports my assertion that some Asian women might be different from other non-Asian women you might date. Someone not born in the United States with immigrant parents is going to differ from someone born and raised in America. Of course, there are countless Asian-American women who have assimilated into American culture so well that she will be no different from other women in the U.S. However, many women, particularly the ones who arrived after 1990, might be different. They will be more in tune with their Asian heritage and have Asian values, which I will describe later in this book.

Just because an Asian woman is an immigrant does not mean she cannot speak English or know American culture. A thirty-year old woman who immigrated into the U.S. when she was six years old has attended elementary, junior, and high schools and most likely college and often, graduate school in the U.S. Many Asian immigrant women are very accomplished. The people who believe that Asian women are different from non-Asian women are most likely Asian women who have immigrated to the United States from Asia. Some Asian women feel caught between two cultures.

CAUGHT BETWEEN TWO CULTURES

Some Asian women living in the United States, particularly those who grew up here with immigrant parents, are caught between two cultures. Sometimes, their parents are immigrants who came to America due to political and financial hardship and prefer to stick to their traditions. Often Asian women who have such parents strive to assimilate into American society by being outgoing and talkative, only to be criticized by their parents for turning their back on tradition and for being too aggressive in dealing with others.

These women often rebel by completely shunning Asian culture while young, only to discover their roots when they get older. Having to deal with two different standards of behavior can be confusing. If your Asian girlfriend is an immigrant who has experienced the foregoing situation, she might appreciate it if you discuss with her the difficulties of growing up with Asian parents who do not understand American society. If you are an Asian man, discussing the difficulties of being caught between two cultures will bring you and your girlfriend closer together. Some Asian women feel that commonality in cultural background with Asian men results in a higher degree of intimacy that cannot be found with others.

Please keep in mind that I am not saying all Asians are caught between two cultures. Many Asian parents adopt much of American culture and combine it with their own Asian background. Thus, they provide a strong combination of both while raising their children. This is especially true for parents who have grown up in the United States themselves.

Quote from Asian females about their experiences regarding living with two cultures:

> *"As a second generation Chinese American...Raised here in the United States I'm proud to say that although I was taught to respect family and elders, I was also taught the importance of individualism. Few of my Asian friends would consider ourselves shy. Again, I believe it's simply a change in times and generations. In fact while I'm mentioning cultures, I believe that many of us do not even consider the line between the two cultures as existent. The goals and expectations or standards we place upon ourselves are done automatically...whether Asian or not. Naturally, I should add that I come from a community that encourages the sharing of all cultures, yet is still a "whole" community. We all share in the different cultures. I myself speak/read/write Spanish fluently and my Spanish friend speaks/read/write Chinese*

fluently, both of us have traveled to Europe and China...In my mind and I'm sure many would agree women are simply women, whether they be Asian, Hispanic, Caucasian or otherwise. I'd always thought we were all American." Evie.

"Yes, I think Asian women are different. Some are caught between both cultures as I am. And others are Americanized. While still others are in the old world thinking that that I need to worship the ground they walk on and stay two steps behind them because they are older than me and that they are slaves to men." Barbara, age 29, MA.

"The Asian women I'm friends with have had to undergo harsh scrutiny and disapproval from their families if they a) date a non-Asian man, b) decide to move in with a man (Asian or non-Asian!) before marriage, c) date a man the family considers unworthy—"unpromising" career choice, etc. These are all cultural and generational differences, and ones that I've had to go through with my own family. I think how much you allow these pressures to affect your own outlook on dating and relationships is an individual decision." Amy, N.Y.

Note: Some highly Americanized Asian-Americans are not subject to the traditions and values that I had just discussed; also not all Asian-Americans will sooner or later try to find out their roots. Many Asian-Americans never do or care. Asian-American women all have very different levels of "Americanness." The point is that "Asian" is a race category—and that some Asian-Americans are simply well-balanced combinations of both "American" and "Asian" characteristics and others are very "Asian," others completely "American." Therefore, Asians consist of a very diverse community of personalities and backgrounds. You need to be forewarned that indeed there is a big field of cultural things, beliefs and behaviors we can call "Asian" culture but that every single Asian relates to this huge mass of ideas, feelings, behaviors, and philosophies differently. In dating an Asian woman, you have to be sensitive and caring enough to figure out how your Asian girlfriend relates to being "Asian" and how she relates to being "American." Your lady is, above all things, an individual with her own history and identity.

Learn Asian Manners and Etiquette

There are certain rules of etiquette in Asian cultures that many non-Asians do not know about. Know Asian customs to increase your chances with Asian women. I will discuss some of these customs later on in this book.

However, take the time to really learn the customs. For instance, do not confuse politeness with submissiveness. Many Asian women do not talk back to men out of respect for them. This does not mean that these Asian women are pushovers who will let their men do whatever they want with them. In fact, many men report that Asian women are the strongest women they know. Many Asian women are smart when dealing with men, and know how to choose their battles. Rather than picking a lot of fights, a lot of Asian women prefer to let the small things go. Harmony and peace are important parts of Asian traditions, and this is often reflected in every aspect of Asian relationships.

The Importance of Family and Seniority

Asian cultures place a heavy emphasis on family and respecting one's elders. A male reader noticed that 75% of Asian women he met on a particular dating site asked him how close he is to his family and not one non-Asian woman asked him that question. Keep this in mind when you meet an Asian woman's family and make a determined effort to win them over. This will strengthen your relationship with your Asian girlfriend. Also, because of the importance of family in Asian cultures, many Asian women would like to have children when they get married.

Asian Traditions & Interests

Even if your Asian woman has lived in the United States for a long time, Asian attitudes and traditions might influence her thinking to varying degrees. The various Asian cultures are discussed later in this book. For example, karaoke is popular with Asians, so be enthusiastic when going to a karaoke bar.

The Importance of Education

To many Asians, a good education means insurance against poverty. Therefore, from day one, the importance of education has been emphasized in almost every Asian child's mind. Many Asian women prefer educated men with graduate degrees and Ivy League diplomas.

Shyness and Quietness

Asian cultures are implicit instead of explicit, and many things are inferred. Many Asians would prefer to say nothing at all rather than something stupid.

Asian women are broadly considered as being quite shy. When a person enters into a different culture, such as from Asia to the United States, there are many things to adjust to, including the language, food, customs, and so on. Many Asian women do not speak English when they first arrive in the United States, and are thus quietly learning the language. Far fewer American-born or raised, English-speaking Asians are considered shy simply because they can speak the language. In fact, many Asian-Americans are very outgoing.

Another theory holds that Asian women are taught to be quiet. In Asian cultures, respect is valued in daily interactions. Thus, what is often a show of respect gets viewed as shyness. It is true that shyness is a stereotype, but it is sometimes the case that Asian women are very quiet and dignified. If you follow the instructions in this book, do not be surprised if underneath the shy exterior lurks a hot, passionate spirit that will erupt delightfully if you go about things the right way. Do not be discouraged if your Asian date or friend does not act as forward or interested as some of the other women you have known. Some Asian women are shy and, dare I say, old-fashioned when it comes to dating and would rather let the man do the pursuing. Many Asian parents teach their daughters to wait for men to approach them in order not to "lose face." Therefore, be a man about it and pursue an Asian woman ardently!

Finally, you should be careful not to make the Asian woman "shy" away from you by saying things that are a turnoff to her. I say this from experience and from hearing other Asian women's experiences: many men do not know how to talk to Asian women. Read on to learn how!

Why Group All Asian Women Together as a Homogeneous Group?

I have received thousands of emails from men and they all say that they are looking for an Asian woman, as opposed to a Chinese woman, or a Korean woman. It seems to me that men see Asian women as one type of woman that they like, because of their physical characteristics such as delicate features, dark hair, slender builds, and personality traits such as quiet dignity and traditional values. There are similarities between all Asian cultures, and in many ways Asian women are the same, but there are differences between the cultures and between individuals that need to be learned and respected. The U.S. Census and all the dating sites categorize Asians as one group.

Furthermore, some Asians prefer to be grouped together. The politically active students in America's most prestigious universities rallied for Asian-Americans to be treated as one group so that Asians in America could have more political clout. Since Asians are the minority in the United States, whenever some Asians see other Asians on the street, they immediately feel a kinship toward each other. Even though Asians are similar in many ways, they are also different. In the Asian Culture part of this book, I will discuss the various

Are Asian Women Different?

Asian cultures. Also, every individual is different and I do not claim to speak for every Asian woman. Even within individual ethnicities, people differ a great deal.

Many women I interviewed reported that, although they grew up in the United States, men treat them like foreigners, asking if they speak English, offering to show them America. These women feel that being treated like foreigners is a big turnoff. Many women have emailed me and said they just want to be treated like everyone else.

The Asian women I interviewed had the following to say about whether Asian women are different:

Caution When Meeting Men

"I DO think many Asian women are different than other races such as Caucasian, because many of us are more shy & cautious when meeting men, at least I am, and I never put up my photo (I know they say you get fewer replies, which is probably very true), but I just don't feel comfortable having the whole world know I'm looking for a man!! And I need to feel no one I know - knows I've placed an ad as I would feel so uncomfortable if a co-worker saw my ad." Sally, age 32, CT.

Asians Place High Priority on Education, Family and Manners

"Yes, I think the Asian cultures place a very high priority on EDUCATION, FAMILY, MANNERS. PLEASE PASS THIS ALONG TO YOUR MALE READERSHIP." Betty, age 31, VA.

"I'm thinking every culture is different and not everyone follows their culture. Personally I like

learning new things about other cultures. In my family, education is viewed a must. Family is very important and sacrificing for your children is without a thought, your children gets the best then you. Helping them through college is part of the job. Just being understanding is a good way to prolong any type of relationship, if you can't stay in a relationship, then don't start it." May, age 35, CO.

"Yes, we are different. Family is important and they need to understand that family gatherings are important. That food is part of the culture and by making fun of it or refusing to try it is insulting. That following traditions is also very important. What is an odd ritual to them can hold meaning to the people that do the rituals. Respecting the grandparents, parents and greeting them by using their designated title. They should understand the culture and religion and respect it." Yi-Ping, age 26, CA.

Asian Women Speak Out About their Cultural Differences

Many Asian women I spoke to said that men who date Asian women should know about and appreciate Asian culture. These Asian women consider their Asian cultures the main reason why they consider themselves to be different. Also, many Asian women consider themselves to be more sensitive than other women.

"There are culture differences for all people. I had to explain to my ex's how to act and behave when meeting my parents." Linda, age 28, RI.

"I guess growing up in America, where kids are kids and they don't understand, you try to uphold yourself, you know? It's important to understand any given culture, but yes, many times the Asian culture is overlooked, or made fun of. To get the understanding

of each other is important, regardless of what your background is. It is nice if they understand." Virginia, age 34, D.C.

"Yes, they need to understand the culture and show some respect. Depending on the person, people are very sensitive about their cultures. I myself consider being sensitive when it comes to my culture. I might be American-born and raised here all my life, but I took Japanese dancing, Japanese calligraphy, went to Japanese school, currently take Japanese Tea Ceremony classes, etc. When people tell me "What the heck is that" or "Why do you need lessons to prepare tea", etc. etc.... it does upset me. Some don't understand when I explain so I just don't bother." Noriko, age 34, CA.

"Yes, before a man dates an Asian woman, he should do research and take some history and language classes so he can communicate and be cognizant of her culture and then he can realize the whole realm of a completely different world that will open up to him. The mystique is because of his ignorance. Once he passes that ignorance, he can really decide if this is a mystique that he really wants to be a part of his life. And all Asian cultures are completely different. He should learn this and learn it well." Helen, age 40, NY.

"I think we are deeper and need more sensitivity and support." Debbie, age 23, AZ.

"Yes, just like any other race difference. Being race sensitive is important to me, just so that you don't offend your 'partner'." Sylvie, age 26, WA.

"Not only because they are dating Asians, but when you date anyone outside of your own culture or race, you have to be a bit educated about what culture, they are from, it may be very same as yours." Christie, age 27, CA.

CHAPTER 2

WHY MEN PREFER ASIAN WOMEN

Go on the Internet and check out some Asian women-white/black male dating clubs such as those on Yahoo.com and you'll think these guys are members of a cult worshipping supreme beings they call Asian females. There are many men seeking Asian women, and they seek them for various reasons. Many men prefer the Asian look: the dark hair, light skin, almond-shaped eyes, and often-slender bodies of Asian women. Other reasons men give for preferring to date Asian women include cultural and emotional compatibility and the possibility of having good-looking children with Asian women. Some people (mostly those who oppose Asian and Caucasian relationships, and/or interracial relationships and marriages) believe that men prefer Asian women because they are submissive. This does not seem to be the case, according to my research. I did a poll on my website, www.AttractAsianWomen.com, and asked people why they preferred Asian women. Out of the 400+ respondents to this poll (at the time of this writing), 41% said that they like Asian women because "They look good;" 32% chose "They are sexy;" 11% picked "I am Asian myself;" 10% picked "They have nice personalities;" 4% chose "I can't score with other women;" and only 2% chose "They are submissive."

My friends tell me that it is not easy to meet an Asian woman. An Asian female friend of mine once placed an ad in the paper and in one week received 200 responses from mostly very eligible men.

Yes, Asian women are popular these days, thanks in part to Asian media stars. More and more people are starting to learn what many Asian women fans have known for years: Asian women are beautiful and powerful, and you will be very lucky to get one as your girlfriend. I was just browsing through Internet personal ads the other day, and this woman had put up the caption: ASIAN WOMAN HERE! As research for this book, I clicked on her ad. She turned out not to be Asian, but she wrote, "But I made you look!" signaling the popularity of Asian women with men on the Internet.

For a list of reasons why a certain Caucasian man dates Asian women, go to the Asiaphiles and Sellouts site (<u>http://members.tripod.com/~scipoet/why.htm</u>).

The Caucasian Webmaster of this site lists the reasons why he dates Asian women, which includes the feeling that Asian women are attracted to him. It is true that you tend to date those women who send out signals that they are attracted to you. Another factor listed on this site is that it is more culturally acceptable for a Caucasian man to date an Asian woman than a black or Hispanic woman.

According to Tanaka Tomoyki, in "Disparity in Asian/white Interracial Dating FAQ", (http://cs.indiana.edu/hyplan/tanaka/disparity/disparity.txt), some of the reasons that men prefer Asian women include:

1. Asian females' attractiveness is enhanced by the "sexist" ideal of beauty, which includes such physical characteristics such as youthfulness and slimness. Asian women tend to look younger and thinner than other women, and therefore, men tend to prefer them for girlfriends and wives.

2. War brides and businessmen brides factor: Businessmen and soldiers who have traveled to Asia frequently develop a preference for Asian women and often bring back Asian wives.

Consider the following quote from one of my male readers:

> *"I have been all over Asia as a military man and as a result have become very attracted to Asian women and cultures. Most of all, I really became attracted to Filipina women."* Jack, age 32, PA.

According to a posting on Delphiforums.com by a Caucasian woman who speaks Chinese, studied Chinese Culture, and married a Chinese man, (http://forums.delphiforums.com/asianwhite/start) theory on why some men are more sensitive than others, and thus prefer to date women from cultures that value family, tradition, education, and respect. This lady wrote that sensitive men are naturally drawn to Asian women because the women appreciate them for who they are. She indicated that as Elaine N. Aron writes in her book, *The Highly Sensitive Person*, the inherited trait (a function of the nervous system) of sensitive people, is found in 15-20% of all higher animals. She quotes Ms. Aron as claiming in her book that this trait is not fully appreciated in American society, as American culture often expects men to be outgoing and less sensitive, but is appreciated in Asian cultures. In summary, the lady on Delphiforums.com stated that sensitive men are more appreciated in Asian society and thus some sensitive men are drawn to Asian cultures. This is a very interesting theory regarding why men prefer Asian women.

I went on Amazon.com to read about *The Highly Sensitive Person*, and in the book description section, highly sensitive people are said to have keen imaginations and vivid dreams. Come to think of it, men who have written to me about Asian women seemed to be highly sensitive.

Consider the following quotes by my male readers:

> *"In the past few years I have had closer friendships than before with Asian guys and gals, just by circumstance. Since I am a lover of cultures I have been learning about Asian (mostly Chinese) culture*

from them. I used to think of Asian people as quiet, hard-working people who mostly kept to themselves - possibly because my interactions were almost entirely on the commercial level with Asian immigrants who didn't have the English fluency and/or the time for in-depth conversations about cultural issues. What I have discovered from my male and female friends, who have responded so warmly and positively to my inquisitiveness, is a great similarity in values and family structure to my own Jewish background. I have discovered philosophical and religious beliefs, which are compatible with personal beliefs I've always held. And (at the risk of sounding stereotypical) there is usually a certain type of behavior/decorum/manner among Asians I've known, met, and observed which I find mirrors how I was raised: a certain way of carrying oneself – not being loud and obnoxious, observing basic manners and courtesies, not embarrassing one's family by engaging in bad behavior; in a word:"respect." Possibly growing out of this, I also find Asian women to be physically attractive. I sense a certain sweetness, strength, and down-to-earth nature in their personalities." Bob, age 45, CA.

"*I have always been attracted to Asian females, there is no way to really explain why. One person I know says I must have been Japanese, or Chinese or some other race or Asian in a past life or several past lives. Who knows? My family says I should have been born an Asian since I like them so much. I always tell them to be careful what they say, plastic surgery can do great things these days! They get real quiet after that! HE HE HE !!! I love to yank their chains any time I can . But I never do it out of meanness, they just have their own ideas of who I should date, marry and have kids with (basically a white blonde , with blue eyes, etc...) I tell them to get over it cuz it ain't happening!*

I think personally Asian/white babies are the cutest of them all, and I have seen the results of when they grow up! One of my childhood friends in Oregon is half Japanese/half white and I always would walk up to her and say:"HUBBA HUBBA!!" She'd always giggle over it but her dad scared the hell out of me as a teen, he is a registered samurai for Japan. He used to scare all of the guys that came to date his daughter! I used to laugh about it when I'd see him at work, he'd always come out dress in traditional kimono, hair pulled back, the works. He'd strut out of his dojo with his katana in his waistband walk around the guy with one hand on the scabbard frowning at the guy staring him down, and I'd be in the background laughing till my side ached! He even made one guy pee in his pants and go home running." Ken, age 32, NV.

"One of my friends brought my picture to her Father in Beijing (he is a Chinese doctor - herbalist, and also he does some fortune telling and some other stuff). She told him nothing about me. He said that I was Chinese in previous life. I read a story on your site, where the guy says that maybe he was Chinese in his previous life, but THIS looks for real. When it comes to China, any new information I found out, whether reading a book or talking to people always seemed NOT new. It always felt like I just remembered something that I already knew. Many times, I would hear some things from Chinese people, I know that they are lying. A lot of times Chinese people do not tell the truth to "Lao Mei" (Americans), and I always knew, when they are lying, even if I knew nothing about the subject. Since 12 years old, I have been attracted to Chinese women...not Korean, not Japanese, not Thai, but Chinese. When I was 12 I knew nothing about China or Chinese women, yet I felt some kind of pulling towards China...See, I am not one of those men. It is different with me." Todd, D.C.

"I am very attracted to Asian women and the only women I am interested in pursuing are Asian women. I like how Asian women look, but I also feel like I have a more loving (non-sexual) connection with them. I am Jewish and my family is upset that I won't date Jewish women and almost exclusively date Asian women. I really don't care about that because I want to live my life and dating Asian women makes me happy." Adam, age 34, NY.

"Some men like blonde hair, blue eyes; I like dark hair, dark eyes." Rod, age 38, NJ.

CHAPTER 3

SHOULD YOU PUT HER ON A PEDESTAL?

Men email me all the time asking me to set them up with their "Asian Princess." "She is out there, and I must find her," one guy told me. This guy has gone on over twenty dates in the past month in search of his "Asian Princess." Who is this "Asian Princess" and does she really exist?

In the realm of Asian fantasy women, I believe there exists three types of Asian women men fantasize about:

The Geisha: The Geisha started as the exotic Japanese woman who entertained men for money, and became the Asian woman who would do anything to please her man. The Geisha girl business is out of date. It's colonial era stuff that Hollywood perpetuated before my time.

The Asian Sex Goddess: The Asian Sex goddess is the Ling in *Ally McBeal*-type. She is what men like to see on television, but men are too scared of her to have a relationship with her, let alone marry her. Men are really looking for their "Asian Princess."

The Asian Princess: She is the woman of every man's dreams. Men who cultivate this fantasy have observed the emergence of Asia as a world economic power and have noticed many modern Asian-

Americans who attend the best high schools and colleges. They also feel disillusioned (and perhaps have been shot down) by liberated modern American women who will not put up with disrespectful treatment. These men have turned out a substitute girl on a pedestal, a.k.a. the "Asian Princess," who they hope is anxious to please (Geisha carry over) and still impressed with American men. This "Asian Princess" is imagined by men as being flawless and perfect. Her mind and motives are in the heavens all the time, and she is always freshly showered and never, ever picks her nose or belches. She is the perfect mother, interested in just pure romantic love. The "Asian Princess" on a pedestal is sweeter and more loving than the sex goddess, who is lustful and animalistic. A man wants to protect his "Asian Princess." It used to be part of the myth that the male offered protection, but this "protector" role is increasingly being recognized as unrealistic—and often demeaning to women. Perhaps some men are looking for their "Asian Princess" to once again be able to protect. One guy wrote to me: "When I find my Asian Princess, I want to save her from the world."

Consider the following men who seem to have fantasies of Asian women who do not really exist:

One guy told an Asian female friend of mine that he prefers Asian women to other women because "Asian women are less materialistic." I have news for this guy: Some Asian women might be more polite in some ways, but they are not any less materialistic than anyone else. For example, there was a certain Filipina who had over 1,220 pairs of shoes.

Another Caucasian businessman said to my Asian female friend that he prefers Asian women to other women because he " can date a brunette without being shot down." This man met my Asian female friend through the personals, but did not want to meet her until he got a better idea of what she was really like (i.e. was she the "Asian Princess" of his dreams?). So he kept on calling her and they had hours and hours of conversation. Finally, she got bored and started to tease him about the way he talked, which she thought was humorous and cute. She was just being her funny, Asian-American self. She never heard from him again. I guess she was not the "Asian Princess" he was seeking.

Many men in New York like to attend the "Asian and American" parties advertised in the Assortments section of *New York* magazine. The Asian and American matchmakers organize these parties to bring more clients to their matchmaking business.

"We go to all of the Asian and American parties; we want the women of Flushing," declared one gentleman. "We do not want to attend those Asian college girl parties."

What does this tell me? That some men do not want to date the liberated Asian-American girls who are well-educated in the United States and who are like American women. That they are less intimidated by recent immigrant women, who often reside in Flushing, Queens in New York.

Could it be that men are so scared of the modern American woman—a category that includes more "American" Asian-Americans—that they want the kinder and gentler (they think) "Asian Princess"? And, is this so wrong?

The guy who I mentioned before who went on twenty dates in a month searching for his "Asian Princess" wants something that seems very hard to find: an "Asian Princess" who is Americanized. But she is out there, he is sure.

What does it mean to be an "Asian Princess who is Americanized"?

Asian princess = perfect, romantic, polite, pretty, soft, kind.
Americanized = knowledgeable about American culture, speaks decent English, has a good job (so that it signals cultural attainment and intelligence), and has lived in the U.S. long enough to have all of the above.

Is it possible for an Americanized Asian woman to be romantic, soft and kind? I believe so. However, do watch that you face reality and see your Asian girlfriend as a person and not as a perfect princess because she is a human being. It is suffocating for a woman to be a perfect figurine all the time.

Some men prefer their "Asian Princess" NOT to be Americanized, as we see in Mr. "We Want the Women of Flushing." See also, MrAsiaphile.com, which states that members of MrAsiaphile.com do not want Asian-Americans (which I interpret to mean they do not want liberated, Americanized Asian women who are like their non-Asian counterparts).

From articles written by people against men with the "Asian fetish," it seems some people think men are looking for something exotic and set impossible standards for an "Asian Princess." Some of the qualities these people accuse men of looking for include:

THE SUBSERVIENT ASIAN
THE SEXY ASIAN

For those men looking for the subservient Asian, they should know that most Asian women in the United States are not subservient. Subservient is often used to describe Asian women who date non-Asians, reminiscent of the white man colonizing poor Asian countries. However, Asian women who date non-Asians sometimes do so because they are rebelling against the Asian way of life, not only of men, but also of a society that dominates women. Can a woman be rebellious and subservient at the same time? Some Asian women complain that Asian culture expects them to be subservient to men, and some Asian women do not marry within their own ethnicities simply because that is expected of them. In the year 2002, women in rural China and elsewhere in Asia are still undereducated and are expected to plow the fields as agricultural laborers. Many women in Asia do the work that men do not want to do. I know of many Asian women/non-Asian men relationships where the woman is more dominating and aggressive than the man.

I have also read article after article criticizing Asian women for dating outside their race as if these women didn't know any better.

To think that Asian women are clueless when they enter into relationships is to insult their intelligence. When an Asian woman dates someone, whether Asian or non-Asian, she is exercising her freedom of choice. It was not so long ago that even freedom of marriage was not allowed of Asian women, and they were forced to marry whomever their parents chose for them. My brother used to scare away my would-be suitors by (jokingly) telling them that I was with my "arranged." In this multicultural society, a melting pot of nations, perhaps the best policy is to be open-minded and let love find us wherever it may find us.

Take a look at the *New York Times* Weddings section on Sunday, May 12, 2002, and you will see that not one, but TWO Caucasian women have married Asian men recently. Contrary to popular belief, Asian women are not the only ones marrying outside the race. According to a study done by the University of Michigan School of Social Research (http://www.umich.edu/~newsinfo/Releases/2000/Mar00/r032300a.html), 21.3% of Asian men in the U.S. are married to non-Asian women and a whopping 46.4% of Asian men are co-habitating with non-Asian women. The reason why Asian women get all the blame for marrying outside the race is perhaps because the media likes to concentrate on what will get people's attention. Asian women and white men, oh how controversial and sexy! Beware of all the Asian women stealing all our good white men, think the people who control the media. There is very little chance of that happening. According to the study I just cited, 95.9% of white men marry white women and 94.6% of white men co-habitate with white partners.

> *"Some Asians are sensual and do take care of their men. But depending on their upbringing, they can also just look Asian, but have become Americanized in their ways and thinking. Like I say buyer beware when looking for the "Subservient Asian." Diane, age 25, CO.*

As for men looking for women they find sexy, isn't sexual attraction what dating and mating is all about? However, note that many, if not most, Asian women do not want to be viewed as and treated like exotic sex objects.

CHAPTER 4

WHAT ASIAN WOMEN THINK OF GUYS WHO HAVE THE "ASIAN FETISH"

Several Asian women I interviewed enjoy the attention they are getting from men with the "Asian fetish." However, many Asian women hate men with the "Asian fetish." Many Asian women do not want to be treated as exotic sex objects. Actually, a lot of people do not like the term "Asian fetish" because of the sexual connotations associated with it. Many people believe a fetish to be an obsession of a sexual nature with an object, such as a foot or shoe fetish. Therefore, some people prefer to call it a preference; some men prefer Asian women. This is also known as "Asiaphilia," a love of Asian culture, women, etc. However, the term "Asian fetish" is used to describe the intense devotion some individuals have toward Asian people. Many people object to the term "Asian fetish." Here is what one male reader wrote:

> "I think there's a massive, huge difference between such a fetish and my preference for Asians. I can point to some very specific reasons why I like Asian women. I believe Asian women have a certain sense of grace, which is wonderful and very appealing—before I got to know Asians well, I didn't really understand what the word "grace" really meant. I think they understand better than most Americans what it takes to create harmony in one's family, workplace and community. There are also things I don't like about many Asians,

but on balance, I still am very much drawn to Asians and women of Asian origin. (I also am drawn to Latina women for a different set of reasons.) I just think this is very, very different from any fetishes I have." Ted, age 35, WA.

Critics argue that men with the "Asian fetish" objectify Asian women. Numerous Asian women resent that they are viewed as sexier and expected to perform better in bed just because they are Asian. Perhaps these harsh feelings against men with the "Asian fetish" would lessen if men stop saying ignorant things to Asian women all the time. A lot of men are awkward in their approach, saying to Asian women they have just met on the street such rude things as: "Do you speak English?" and "I like you Orientals." If you are guilty of such crude behavior, stop it, stop it immediately! Show your appreciation of Asian culture and your language skills AFTER you get to know an Asian woman better so you see where she stands in relation to the Asian culture of her parents. When you use Asian language pickup lines on total strangers you are stereotyping and being racially insensitive. DO NOT do it.

Some Asian women I interviewed said they are actually benefiting from the preference for Asian women. After all, you read that there is a man shortage in the United States, and that a woman cannot get a man after age 35. This is probably not true for many Asian woman. In fact, one reader, a 58-year-old Asian lady wrote that she was surprised that she received lots of responses to her ad on the Internet, some even from men a lot younger than her. Is it wrong for some Asian women to like that men prefer them? Critics say that Asian women should not be so happy about the "Asian fetish" because men are just objectifying them. However, it is human nature to want attention, and some Asian women I interviewed are finding it hard to complain when so many men are calling.

What is the difference between liking Asian women for who they are and objectifying them for what they are? In one word: respect. If you behave with respect toward Asian women, and not treat them like exotic sex objects, then you are probably not objectifying them.

What About the "Asian Fetish"?

For example, if you go up to an Asian woman and say "I like you Orientals," you are telling her that you like her for WHAT she is. People want to be liked for who they are and not for what they are.

I get emails from men who, even though they prefer Asian women, do not want to admit that they have an "Asian fetish." This is perhaps due to the bigoted, racist things people say about men who date Asian women. See, for example, Asiaphiles and Sell Outs, http://members.tripod.com/~scipoet/index.html. There are some bad sexual connotations that come to some people's minds when one mentions "Asian fetish." One Asian lady I interviewed said that men with the "Asian fetish" expect Asian women to be sex-craved housekeepers. Many Asian women are offended that they are wanted simply because they are Asian, and want to be treated like real people instead.

Just look on the Internet and you will see numerous clubs for Asiaphiles, including males interested in Asian females and females interested in Asian males.

Non-Asian men—and Asian men as well—should ultimately accept each Asian woman for who she is. Accept her for her own distinctive combination of "Asian" and "American" cultural traits. Perhaps it is impossible to get away from this tendency to objectify, but that once we get to know someone, we have got to get past this tendency and look at our mate as a person, with her or his own history, background, "Asian" and "American" cultural background, and so on.

QUOTES FROM ASIAN WOMEN WHO LIKE MEN WITH A PREFERENCE FOR ASIAN WOMEN

"Finally they get their senses right! lol...Asians are the most beautiful women out there! (especially me...wOoohahahaha)" R.R., age 20, NJ.

"Asian Fetish? Do you mean by just us being Asian?....I dunno, I love it.??? Hey....I mean damn...it's more for me!!!...and all the white loving Asian women out there!" T.C., age 19, NY.

"Hmm, I don't know. I guess they try to treat you much better than they would anyone else. It's almost like bribery." M.M., age 30, CA.

"Those men have excellent taste. Why settle for less?" T.R., age 20, CA.

"It has been working to my advantage, so I'm not complaining." Jen, age 30, CT.

"The men with the "Asian fetish" adore their women, which is what I like. I would definitely prefer to date men with the "Asian fetish"." Fay, age 35, TX.

"They all want me...but they can't get me since I'm seeing 2 men already...and I have a high taste which makes some men hard 2 get at me." Delia, age 19, NY.

"They have always been very attentive and caring and make you feel as if you are the most beautiful woman in the world." LiFei, age 24, CT.

"We look better I guess? It's definitely not boob size!" Nancy, age 25, NY.

Quotes from Asian Women Who Have a Live and Let Live Attitude About Men Who Prefer Asian Women

"That's perfectly fine. It's a preference. Some like blondes or brunettes. I prefer White Italian men over any other race." Sandy, age 24, NY.

"I am a bit flattered for me and for all Asian women but I don't want to appear attractive to a man simply for my race. It's nice to know he also looks for the individuality, personality and characteristic as well." Bebe, age 34, CT.

"Asian fetish? It's a trend. I've read an article on a Website that indicated that gay Asian men are the new "eye candy" in the gay community. On The View, Lisa Ling introduced Asian men as the newest and hottest import. At times I am convinced that American men have an Asian fetish because of their endearing "all American macho" syndrome. They perceive Asian women as exotic creatures, as well as more passive/submissive. Madame Butterfly, Farewell my Concubine ~~ even Asian men are more exotic and passive." Suki, CA.

"I don't see it as a fetish. Just a preference." A.D., age 27, CT.

"Personally I don't care... if that's their thing...that's their thing." Lumi, age 29, AZ.

"Well, being that I have my "strong preferences" as well, I really don't think it's fair that I comment on this subject, although ... I'm not out "hunting" down long haired (Asian or Latino) muscular musicians either. I wish I could but, I'm too much of a scaredy-cat, and being labeled a "stalker" would probably freak me out - LOL." Q.C., age 30, CA.

"Well, I guess the Asian fetish is good for the FOBS (those who just came to the USA from Asia) or Asian-American girls (those who were born or grew up in the USA), since they are usually the ones who have much interest in dating white men. Personally, I don't have much opinion on Asian fetish. However if this *person has a really bad case, like to the point he practically thinks that "he" is Asian. Then I think that's kind of sad. No one race is better then another really. It's good you admire another race or culture, but don't forget who you are."* Betty, age 34, NY.

"Um...I think it's like how some white women like black men only. It's just an issue of preference. The Asian race isn't superior to any other race; all races are equal." Haley, age 28, NY.

"My experience with men who has Asian Fetish has been no different that any other guy I have encountered with." Li Fan, age 34, NY.

"Different people have different preferences. I myself would prefer Asian men." Giselle, age 28, MI.

"I think it's pretty crazy, but whatever suits them is cool with me. I pretty much just date white guys........is that a Caucasian fetish?" Susan, age 26, CA.

"I've dated a few but, never fell in love with them (not even in lust)." Estella, age 29, WA.

"Everyone has their own preference when it comes to dating so there is nothing wrong with that." Bebe, age 34, NY.

"I don't know why some men prefer Asian women only. I guess it is we all want what we cannot have and variety is the spice of life. I bet lot of Asian guys prefer only Caucasian girls too. I don't prefer Asian guys either." Whitney, age 23, CA.

Quotes from Asian Women Who Think Asian Women Have Been Negatively Affected by the Preference for Asian Women/ "Asian fetish"

"Men who target Asian women for relationships just because they are Asians are offensive to me regardless of whether or not they verbalize how attracted they are to Asian women." Anonymous.

"I think that some guys that have Asian fetish just believe in that rumor that Asian women have a wild side...how we all look very innocent and yet in the bedroom we're like animals...I really don't know." Nancy, age 30, VA.

"Interesting but not sure I understand it or trust it...it has bad sexual connotations." Tammy, age 30, NY.

"The only reason my ex-boyfriend (a white guy) dated me is because I was Asian. I found this out after we had broken up. He told me that if I weren't Asian and still the same person he would not have even glanced my way. Then there's my friend J..he's a black guy..he loves Asian girls. I'm his "Asian girl advisor." He told me that his reason for the "Asian fetish" is because the only girl who ever made him feel like someone was Asian. I guess he's trying to relive the memories." Michelle, age 28, CA.

"I don't like been deemed as "an Asian chick." I'm a person too. I have feelings, personality, a life. It's kind of annoying the "Asian fetish." I mean I would like someone to like me NOT just because I was Asian...but for who I am." Laoni, age 29, HI.

"They just always treat me so well, like they've just won a goddess and then I get sick of it because it seems

they wanted me as a statue of beauty to show off and not for my mind or "WHO" I am rather "WHAT" I am." Helen, age 27, NY.

"They're very persistent to see how 'wild' you get in the bedroom." Lori, age 24, NY.

"Seems most of them have some kind of fantasy that they want fulfilled." Tina, age 30, AZ.

"Not good, they will date another Asian woman if the other Asian woman has more Asian features then yourself. They will also drop you if the other Asian woman is into having sex immediately." Tara, age 32, NY.

"A lot of guys think that just because I am Asian, they assume things about me, which has been both good and bad in the past." Aimee, age 29, CA.

"I still think American men are uneducated about the Asian mystique because Asian people as a whole still shy away from them and keep them ignorant of their true cultures. There are many men married to Asian women and I don't think they have learned either the language or the traditions, either by choice or the family finds it unnecessary to educate them. So a lot still remains outside of the cultures. Things are slowly changing though. I can see some influences filtering in. Also Asians are also shy about imposing their doctrines on other cultures." Dawn, age 34, VA.

"They are stupid and ignorant." Anonymous.

"Hey, if that's their preference, I am cool about it, but there are some guys who are jerks and date Asians for stupid reasons and I think that would be uncool." Aki, age 22, CA.

"I think it's overrated, but sometimes understandable. We're all females, some tend to stray or just do things that aren't "typical", but it's just a phase. Or it's just some feeble-minded excuse for Lord knows what..." Li-Fan, age 32, NY.

"I have heard of it but I think some of the men who are into it are in fantasyland." Natalie, age 28, HI.

"For Asian guys, it looks natural. When it comes to the Caucasian Asian fetish, it seems some of these Caucasian men are not competitive for Caucasian women. Like too small, less educated or dominant for women etc. I think only good case would be a Caucasian guy who knows much about the Asian culture like able to speak the language, like Asian foods, traveled etc." Chris, age 23, IL.

"I personally have no problem with it, but many women have complained to me about exclusive race dating seeing that dating should consist of looks as well as personality." Stacy, age 23, HI.

"I think it's crazy. I certainly don't want any man dating me just because I am Asian. I want him to date me because of who I am really am inside." Danielle, age 28, CA.

"Luckily, I haven't dated any of those. I do have a guy friend who has the "Asian fetish." We argue about it all the time. I tell him it's wrong, and he tells me that there's nothing wrong with it." Julie, age 23, NY.

"I think "Asian Fetish" is a bit overrated. Some "Asians" are sensual and do take care of their men. But depending on their upbringing, they can also just look Asian, but have become Americanized in their ways and thinking. Like I say buyer beware when looking for the "Subservient Asian." Diane, age 25, CO.

"Most men with the "Asian Fetish" want to get you in bed and they let their attraction be known. But sometimes I feel that they have a preconceived picture in their head that they don't take you for who you really are, they are just concentrating on you being "Asian" and that Asian women tend to be subservient. It's almost like I am being viewed as a Sex Craved Housekeeper willing to cook, clean and do whatever they say." Diane, age 25, CO.

"I won't choose those types of guys for my boyfriend and hopefully I would like to avoid having friends like that. If they love Asian culture, they are supposed to have more Asian male friends. Only after they have Asian male friends should they start looking for their Asian girl friends. I feel it is more likely to insult for the sex of woman and Asian culture allow men to do so without doing so." Minna, age 24, NY.

"This white guy was a kind of this type and I didn't think about him as a boyfriend even he was a professor of a famous college and mentally and financially attractive." Crissy, age 25, CA.

"Hmm...I'm not sure...its good in some ways...like...different kinds of guys are more interested in Asian women...but...it is also bad in another way...like...a lot of times...guys with the "Asian fetish" like you JUST because you are Asian...and figuring out if he likes you becuz of YOU...or if he likes u becuz YOU ARE ASIAN...really is a bitch. Ahhh...the "Asian fetish" guys...uhhh....good and bad...I guess it depends more on each guy...like this one guy I met from my English 102 class...he was one hot mother...he was an "other" ..a mix I think...South American and white....we called him the Asianluver...he had a mad case of the Asian fetish...he liked ALL Asian girls...as long as they were remotely attractive. But...he wasn't all bout being

Asian...he was more for a girl ..like the person she was inside too......on the flip side...this other guy I met in my math 275 class...this black guy...oh my lord...all he did was stalk and try to grope every Asian girl on campus..and after while....all the Asian girls...even if they hated each other...helped and rescued each other from him...it was so sick...he would always go around saying.."My life-long goal and dream is to marry an Asian woman and move to her country and have as many babies as possible" ..when he said 'an Asian woman'...he really meant any Asian woman...blah!" Connie, CA.

"Some were real sweet and can't get over the fact that we are so beautiful and exotic. And others were losers who expected Asian chicks to be all submissive." Tara, age 34, KY.

"I think it is downright stupidity. It's okay to prefer Asian women, but you shouldn't limit your women to just us. You never know who you'll run into." Anonymous.

"They're overtly obsessed. Too much..."Oh I loooooove Asian this and that..." Get over it. Besides, I'm a five foot ten Asian woman. Not your typical petite Asian/ China doll." Annette, age 24, CA.

"The severe ones talk non-stop about Chinese food, Asian cultures and countries, good way to make me feel out of place and foreign, it's not fair, we don't look at you and start talking about McDonald's French fries and burgers." Rita, age 29, NY.

"Men with the Asian fetish are annoying and obvious. Men wanting to know where I'm from, if I speak the language, they know someone who speaks an Asian

language (not even the one I'm talking about). Saying they know someone who was Asian, their last girlfriend was Asian. It's retarded and a big turn-off." Missy, age 23, HI.

"They think that Asian woman are always trying to please their mate always, and believe in the rumor about Asians being freaks." Paulette, age 28, MA.

"I think that's their preference as long as they don't prefer it just because they think we make good housewives. And because we are supposedly good wives that listen to their husbands. If they like Asians because of their beauty and their minds then that's fine, but not because they want a maid." Marie, age 35, CA.

CHAPTER 5

DO ASIAN WOMEN FIND NON-ASIAN MEN ATTRACTIVE AND DO THEY WANT TO DATE THEM?

It depends. Men of all races have desirable qualities. Love and attraction depend on individual women's preferences. This chapter explores the popular topic of Asian and Caucasian (as well as other) relationships.

Some Asian and African-American men have complained that white men get all the Asian women, that everywhere you look on the street, there is another Asian female-Caucasian male couple. White men constitute the majority of men in the United States, and perhaps this is the reason for the perception that there are more white men dating and marrying Asian women than any other group in the United States. According to the U.S. Census, Caucasian husband/Asian wife couples are the most common interracial couples in the United States. A study by the University of Michigan's Institute for Social Research (cited in Ben Chan's "Why Asian Women Don't Date Asian Men", available at http://www.jademagazine.com/10pr_revelations.html) revealed that 25% of married Asian women have Caucasian husbands. Also, almost 45% of cohabitating Asian women live with Caucasian partners, while less than 43% live with Asian men. On the other hand, 96% of white women have white husbands and 93% of cohabitating white women live with white men. 96% of African-American women have African-American husbands and 94% of cohabitating African-American women live with African-American men. Why are so many Asian women dating and marrying out of their race?

There seems to be a strong mutual attraction between Asian females and Causcasian males. An Asian female reader made the observation that there are more varieties of white men from which to choose. According to the Asiaphiles and Sellouts site (http://members.tripod.com/~scipoet/why.htm), Asian women and white men date each other because of reciprocal attraction. Men tend to date those women who are attracted to them. Another factor listed on this site is that it is more culturally acceptable for a Caucasian man to date an Asian woman than a black or Hispanic woman.

Some Asian women felt that white men were the only ones interested or brave enough to approach them. The problem reported by many Asian women who would rather date Asian men is that there are few available and eligible Asian men. In fact, many Asian women said that Asian guys, if they can be found, never ask them out. For example, see "The Asian-American Woman's Burden," by Nadine Park Brookston, available on http://www.goldsea.com/Features/Comments/woman.html. However, many Asian men have emailed me asking to be introduced to Asian ladies. According to the *Washington Post*, 36% of young Asian-American men born in the United States marry white women. According to the above-cited study done by the University of Michigan Institute for Social Research, 78.7% of married Asian men have Asian wives and 53.6% of co-habitating Asian men have Asian partners. This study also shows that 15.8% of Asian men are married to white women, and 37.3% of Asian men are living with white women. The percentage of Asian men with interracial partners is high compared with black and white men. 95.9% of white men have white wives and 94.6% of white men are living with white women. 89.8% of African-American men have African-American wives and 83.6% of African-American men are cohabitating with African-American women. Many Asian male members of my website Asiansocials.com report that they once were only interested in white women, but have recently come to appreciate the allure of Asian women. Some of my Asian male friends only date African-American women. Many Asian men also date and marry non-Asian women.

Some Caucasian men have mentioned that the Asian women they know only want to date Asian men. While it is true that some Asian women prefer Asian men, I estimate around 70% of the hundreds of Asian women I interviewed are interested in non-Asian men. Many of these women are also interested in Asian men. Some of the less Americanized women stated that while they would like to date non-Asian men, they fear that they will not be compatible with the men due to differences in culture. Nonetheless, these women would like to learn more about American culture so that they can date American men. The number one reason for not wanting to date non-Asian men was that non-Asian men tend to put down Asian men or say other rude things when approaching Asian women.

Another reason for dating Asian men is the desire to please the parents. Some Asian parents prefer their daughters to marry Asian men. However, nowadays, most Asian parents are more open-minded about their daughter's chosen mate. For a non-Asian, this is particularly true if you can win them over with your charming personality and sincere effort to be accepted into the family. Other members of your Asian girlfriend's family will probably be more open-minded than her parents. However, this may not be true if they are totally against Asians dating non-Asians. One Filipina I interviewed stated that a good way to win the family over is through the children, such as nieces or nephews of your girlfriend. Children are probably less prejudiced, and if they like you, they will sing your praises and convince other members of the family to invite you over again. Toys and candy are always welcomed. I will give you more advice on dealing with an Asian woman's family later on in this book.

Many Asian women I interviewed enjoy socializing with other Asian women, because they feel a connection toward one another. What is their favorite topic of conversation? The weird things non-Asian men say to them on the street. When Asian women go out, they often go out in groups. I met many Asian women while doing research for this book, I received quite a few invitations to hang out with my Asian female interviewees. My point is, if you make friends with some Asian women, they can introduce you to their other Asian female friends.

Reasons Why Some Asian Women Only Date White Men

In my interviews with Asian women who exclusively date Caucasian men, the most common reason stated for dating them was physical attraction. They prefer the physical features of white men, such as blond hair, blue eyes ("like a Ken doll"), Italian features, and so on. One Asian lady even said she likes white men for their "exotic" look. Well, in Asia all white people are exotic-looking. I remember an incident as a 4-year-old in Taiwan. I was hanging out with four of my little buddies when all of a sudden we saw a Caucasian guy about age 30. We chased him down the street yelling "*Meiguoren! Meiguoren!*" ("American! American!"). The poor guy was so scared that he climbed over a wall to escape from us.

Some Asian women stated that they like British, Scottish and Irish accents. Other reasons for dating Caucasian men included wider availability of interested Caucasian men, familarity from growing up in white neighborhoods, and bad experiences with non-Caucasian men. One Asian woman stated that she dates Caucasian men to rebel against her strict parents. Some Asian women report that they date and marry Caucasian men because Asian men are not interested in them, perhaps because they do not fit a specific mold of the ideal Asian female.

Here are some reasons Asian women have given for dating white men:

"White...I have always been attracted to white men...especially Italian men...I love the exotic look...I like to learn about other cultures as well....I feel that Filipino or Asian men have too much in common with me, and are related to me somehow, like a brother." T.S., age 27, NY.

"Usually white. No preference. I guess growing up in a strict household where it's expected to marry Asian,

you tend to rebel and just don't date Asian. Well, at least I was that way, but it's not like I'm not willing to." H.S., age 29, CA.

"White, because I'm attracted to the fact that there are more varieties to choose from." Whitney, age 20, CA.

"I don't date Asian nor Black guys...I prefer to date White or the "other" category....I don't date Asian guys because...most are the ..what I like to call..."Gay-sians" you know what I am talkin about..the kind that think they are better than everyone else..the kind that think they are thugs..but really all they are just confused...the ones that wear their hair, dress, walk , talk the same...I'm not dissing all Asian guys...every once in a while, I'll come across a nice hot Asian guy that is classy, honest, sweet, and unique....and not just another part of the over played cliche that I know as the gaysians...Black guys...there is no attraction... I think they make really great friends....but nothing more than that.It kind of bugs me the way they try to hit on you though...they go about it all wrong.And white guys....I dunno wut it is about them...I'm not talking about all white guys...but the majority of them ...I find very attractive...I guess I just have a white kink." Y.P., age 22, NY.

"I am interested in white men usually (Asians are always too short for me)." Kate, age 27, NY.

"I've dated a lot of different races, but I seem to prefer white guys. I just am most attracted to white guys. That and because I have had bad experiences with Asian guys." Teri, age 30, MI.

"I primarily date white guys. I grew up in an all white town all my life and only dated white guys, this is just the pattern thus far, I would not be closed to someone because of their race." Rose, age 34, VA.

"My first boyfriend was Caucasian when I was 18. I also married him. However, after my divorce, I've dated Asian and Hispanic men, but for some reason, I can relate to the Caucasian men much better. I don't know why." Lia, age 34, NY.

"I've dated all different types and races, and find that white men are the most compatible with me. I first and foremost am very attracted to them, and the vast majority of them hold onto their gentlemanly traditionalism." Dina, age 29, CA.

"White guys because they are gentlemen. I am saying this from experience a lot of other guys play a lot games and think they are players. And only want to date Asian woman because of the rap songs saying how kinky we are." Lisa, age 27, NY.

"White...now. I used to be with other races, but now mainly whites. I just find them more attractive and have more in common with them. More open minded and respectful. Asian men tend to think they should be in charge. White men that I date believe in equality in a relationship." Wendy, age 32, MA.

"I prefer White male because that is what I am attracted to...I can't explain it. I don't know why I am attracted to them, but I am. Light eyes are a big factor." Laura, age 26, CA.

"It depends on where I live. In California, there were a lot of Asians so that's what I dated. Location has a lot to do with who I date. Now that I live in a place where there are more White guys than any other race, I date them." Ling, age 29, AZ.

For more information on Asian and white relationships, go to: http://www.asianwhite.org/

Reasons Why Some Asian Women Prefer Asian Men

Asian women who prefer to date Asian men mentioned feeling a higher degree of intimacy and sharing more in common with Asian men than with other men due to cultural similarities and understanding. The ability for the boyfriend to communicate with their parents and meet the approval of their parents are also important factors in preferring Asian men. Some Asian women report being turned off by white men who tell them negative things about Asian men to make themselves look better. Another Asian female said that she feels that Asian men treat her better and in her experience, non-Asians are too equal in everything (she felt that non-Asians expect to split the check on dates).

Asian guys complain to me that some Asian women turn them down because they are not white men. While it is true that some Asian women only date white men, there are a lot of Asian women who are looking everywhere for Asian men, but cannot seem to find them. I know one beautiful, successful Chinese-American woman in her early 30s who is looking for the following in a mate:

1. He must be stylish.
2. He has to make more money than her.
3. He has to be Chinese or Japanese.

She complains that the Chinese or Japanese guys she meets are either not interested in her or married or not "stylish" enough for her. I asked her what she meant by "stylish" and she said that he has to dress and carry himself in a cool, American way. It seems to me that many Asian women prefer Asian and non-Asian men who are Americanized. This is especially true for Asian women who have lived in the United States for ten years or more and are used to living the American way and dealing with Americans. Recent immigrant women might also prefer "American" or Americanized men because of the incentive to assimilate into American society.

Another attractive Asian female told me that she is an "equal-opportunity" dater, and while she is interested in Asian males, they do not ask her out. I have conducted years of research for this book, and interviewed hundreds of Asian women. The number one complaint Asian women have about Asian men is that Asian men do not ask them out. If you are an Asian man, here is the secret to getting an Asian girlfriend: Ask an Asian woman out today!

To all Asian males: Just be confident and approach lots of women. I know for a fact that many Asian women would love to date Asian men if they only asked. Furthermore, research shows that more Asian women these days are now marrying Asian men.

Quotes from Asian women:

"One more thing on why I wouldn't date white men. This thought just occurred to me, cause some loser just IMed me. I notice white guys have a tendency of putting down Asian men. They say things like "Asian men are small, they have small dick, and etc..." Now, if you're a white guy trying to attract me an Asian girl, and you're talking trash about men of my nationality... Unless you have the IQ of 50, which seems to me most men who have emailed or IMed me, then you should know better than saying something as STUPID as that. That is a MAJOR, MAJOR turn off. Imagine, if I went to a white dude and said something like "Hey Handsome, I know you want me, cause I'm skinny and beautiful unlike some WHITE CHICKS who are FAT." Now do you think this white dude would be "turned on" by a line like that? I didn't think so...And that's why I don't get turn on by white guys, especially those who talk trash about Asian guys. First it shows they're ignorant, 2nd they're rude, and 3rd reason chances are they look down on Asians..so he wouldn't make a good boyfriend, since he probably will look down on me too, and is only using me. (A tip for those Asians in love with white guys.)" Yuni, NY.

"I prefer dating Asian guys but that preference does not put an inhibiting barrier when it comes to other ethnicities. Asian guys present a certain degree of intimacy that cannot be found with others- the food, culture, the language...the ability to communicate with my mother!" Suki, CA.

"I prefer someone that is Asian. I feel they can relate to me better (than non-Asian men), share similar mentality. Also I feel that I can understand them better (then non-Asian men) and how they think because we come from similar backgrounds, and probably share the same beliefs told by parents and grew up with similar rules and manner. Oh yea, if he isn't Asian there would be a next to zero chance of him fitting in with my friends unless he's been "Asians." Meaning, he grew up in an Asian home, with Asian friends, thinks, dress similar to Asian guys. Believe there "IS" a difference." Hillary, NY.

"I've dated my first boyfriend on and off for 5 yrs till sophomore year in college. While dating him, I always wondered how different it would feel to date an Asian guy. Even when we were off, I did not date any Asian guys. I think finally it became such a barrier that we broke up. A few months later, I dated my first Asian guy. It was a definitely different experience. There was a certain extra degree of intimacy involved because of the common language and culture. After we've broken up, I began to realize that ethnicity and culture do play an essential role in compatibility. However, I can't seem to find the justification for it. Why should I screen out other guys because of their ethnicity? Therefore...I don't." Eliza, age 28, MA.

"I prefer to date Asian guys...I have dated guys of Spanish descent, but we have too little in common...I feel I have more in common with the guys of Asian ethnicity." Mei Mei, age 30. HI.

"Ideal man? I would say professional Asian male.. funny, sweet, considerate, caring, well-spoken, intelligent.. 5'10", glasses, short spikey black hair, clean cut.. love to travel." Betty, age 24, NY.

"Occupation wise, is not TOO important, as long as he makes enough money to not be stressing about income too much, and also enough to "afford a girlfriend." Not saying that I need a man who'll take me on shopping sprees.. but he needs to be able to do the usual.. But if he's Asian he probably holds that old traditional believe that "girls shouldn't have to pay when they're out with guys." I know it's kind of bad and unfair for men, but hey, I have no problem here, and am used to that kind of treatment. That's why I probably wouldn't date an American or something, because they're too "equal" in everything. I've seen white couples at restaurants split checks right in the middle down to the last penny. To me, I don't mind it occasionally, but then it's just a turn off, and seems like the guy is being kind of cheap." Yuni, age 29, NY.

REASONS WHY SOME ASIAN WOMEN FAVOR AFRICAN-AMERICAN MEN

Asian women who prefer African-American men give reasons such as better lovers, feelings of equality with African-American men, and physical attraction. Some women have remarked that Asian and African-American unions result in the best-looking and most exotic looking children, such as Tyson Beckford, Naomi Campbell, and Tiger Woods. Some Asian girls are more culturally familiar with African-American guys. Also, African-American guys have the appeal of being not only minorities, but also very masculine ones. Thus, the African-American male's status of "minority underdog" and "tough guy" can be very appealing to some Asian women.

Quotes from Asian women:

"I always end up with a black guy. It is not only for a boyfriend. I love black women to have as my friends. So it's more cultural or feeling things, I guess. I feel like we are very equal as a person when I commit with a black guy. That means I could be the one who have to take a role like a man in the relationship sometimes even financially. Asian and some white still require the woman's role. It's only good for money and harmful for my mind." Rosa, age 33, NY.

"Black and Latinos since they make good lovers." Jackie, age 22, NJ.

"I am attracted 2 Black men. wit a fair amount of Income...a job...i like guyz that have an attitude...an ass hole basically! lol. I just like the challenge of breaking them! lol~nice guyz are a turn off...they seem way 2 ez. i like tall guyz...about 6'3" or so. nicely built...hate fat or skinny guyz!!! yuck! I usually date Black men. And Asianz are nice 2...but white guyz? dunno...jush don't catch my interest. I looooooove ghetto guyz! they are sooo cute!!! black guyz seem 2 have more personality...and wat im lookin 4." Ellen, age 21, CT.

"I like black guys because they are handsome and cultured, and I like rebelling against my parents." Mimi, age 25, NY.

For more information on Asian and black relationships, go to the following websites:

Http://clubs.yahoo.com/clubs/blasian

Http://forums.delphiforums.com/n/main.asp?webtag=bumblebees1&nav=start

(Bumblebee: The AfroAsian Online Community)

Http://go.to/blasian.

Http://www.BlackTokyo.com

Why Asian Women Prefer Latino Men

Some Asian women who prefer Latino men say they like qualities common in Latino men such as these men being family-oriented and tradition-based. Some consider there to be a lot of cultural similarities between Asians and Latinos that don't exist between Asians and any other group, and also many differences that make Latinos an "exotic" group for Asian women at the same time. Some ladies reported that they prefer Latino men because these men are more emotional, warm and open-minded.

Quote from an Asian woman:

> *"I prefer American Latino men since they are more family oriented and seems to accept "Asian" ness with less prejudice. They tend to be more emotional and warm which lacked in my family." Jill, age 23, CA.*

> *"I like Spanish men because they are sexy and treat me right." Bebe, age 24, NY.*

Why Race Does Not Matter to Some Asian Women

Many Asian women do not care about the ethnicity of the men they date. To them personality and compatibility matter more. One lady who felt this way said that since she is a single mother Asian men do not accept her and thus she dates men of other races.

Quotes from Asian women:

"I date guys of all races. To me, personality is what matters. The color of someone's skin is not indicative of who or what the person is." Tessa, age 23, NJ.

"Honestly I don't dig Asian guys...they're too traditional for me.. and so are their families. I'm a mother and I know that there are just so many Asian dudes that won't accept me because I have a kid while a whole lot of other races don't really care..but I really have no preference... race is no biggie for me." Mae, age 35, HI.

So Do Asian Women Want to Date Non-Asian Men?

Answer: Some do and some don't!

It really depends on the woman. Each woman has her preference. Regardless of the color of your skin, there are certain things you can do to improve your odds of getting an Asian girlfriend. (Hint: Be brave! Be brave! Be brave!) Read on for more details!

CHAPTER 6

JUST FOR ASIAN MEN

THE GOOD NEWS

Many Asian men write to me after viewing my Website, www.AttractAsianWomen.com. Several of these Asian guys are Asian men who used to date non-Asian women, but are now interested in dating Asian women. Some Asian guys tell me that they are not sure Asian women want to date them. Someone needs to have enough sense to give these Asian men the good news. I will be the one to do so! The good news is: Asian women DO want Asian men! Asian women who prefer Asian men feel that they can relate to Asian men better than non-Asian men due to the similarity in culture both share. Some Asian women believe that their parents and friends would prefer that they date Asian men. One Asian woman declared: "Asian guys present a certain degree of intimacy that cannot be found with others- the food, culture, the language...the ability to communicate with my mother!"

Read for yourself what Asian women have said about Asian men:

"I prefer someone who is Asian. I feel they can relate to me better (than non-Asian men), share a similar mentality. Also I feel that I can understand them better (than non-Asian men) and how they think because

we come from similar backgrounds, and probably share the same beliefs told by parents and grew up with similar rules and manners. Oh yea, if he isn't Asian there would be a next- to- zero chance of him fitting in with my friends unless he's been "Asian." Meaning, he grew up in an Asian home, with Asian friends, thinks, dress similar to Asian guys. Believe me, there "IS" a difference." Hillary, NY.

"I prefer to date Asian guys...I feel I have more in common with the guys of Asian ethnicity." Mei Mei, age 30. HI.

I have received many emails from Asian men who would like my advice on how to attract Asian women. I even gave a Chinese guy advice in Mandarin on how to get a girlfriend. (God, my mother would be so proud of me if she knew.)

I know many Asian women who would love to date Asian men, but cannot seem to find any Asian men who are interested. Here are some tips for an Asian guy to attract more Asian women:

SHOW YOUR INTEREST

- **Smile** — Smiling shows that you are friendly and interested.

- **Eye Contact** — Look deep into her eyes.

- **Be Funny and Vulnerable** — Reveal something vulnerable about yourself to win her heart.

- **Attention** — Look at her, talk to her, call her, and ask her out!

- **Gifts** — Cute little *thoughtful* gifts get her attention. For example, I was very impressed by an Asian guy who brought me a bag of Whoppers (those malted chocolate balls) after I told him I loved them. Really listen to what she says to you, and remember what she said when you buy the presents.

- **Be Stylish** — I am not making this up. More than a few Asian women I interviewed want stylish men. What is the Asian females' definition of stylish?

- **Dress** — Dress stylishly. Read *GQ*, *Maxim*, and other men's magazines. Shop where these magazines suggest.

- **Be Interesting** — Have a wide range of interests. Do interesting things. Be out there, participating in all that life has to offer.

- **Attitude** — My Asian female interviewees who do not date Asian men complain that Asian guys expect them to be the "ideal Asian women": small, thin, humble, smart, pretty, and so on, as if they fell out of a mold.

Also, do not expect an Asian female to be a traditional China Doll who is subservient and there just to cook and clean for you. If you are the modern Asian male who does not expect an Asian woman to be subservient, then let the Asian females you approach know your enlightened attitude, and you will be more attractive to them.

Here is some advice from an Asian-American guy who is very popular with Asian women:

> *"My own tips on Asian women for Asian guys who don't have much luck: I think some Asian guys tend to do bad things that turn off Asian girls, just as non-Asian guys do certain bad things that turn them off as well. I think Asian girls tend to avoid a certain stereotypical Asian male just as strongly as they avoid non-Asian guys with fetishes. They avoid the macho Asian guy who is equally racist and closed-minded as the fetishistic white dude; if you are an Asian guy, be open-minded, tolerant of all races and cultures, and most importantly, develop many diverse interests.*

Be fun and outgoing and show your Asian girl how interesting and offbeat a time you can offer her all the time as her boyfriend by taking her to different kinds of movies—not just cheesy romance flicks, slasher action movies, or the hits of the moment, but indies, foreign and art films, even Asian films by people like Akira Kurosawa, Im Kwon-Taek, and Wong Kar-Wai. Impress her by taking her to concerts, rock shows, fancy restaurants, neat cafes and coffee shops, and other venues that are not typical "Asian" hotspots. Read a variety of books. And be very sensitive both in conversations and in bed; lots of Asian guys suffer from self-centeredness and a dire lack of sensitivity in these and other areas. Lots of Asian girls, I think, are attracted to non-Asian guys because the perception is that non-Asian guys have a more diversified set of interests and hobbies and tend to be more on the sensitive side.

Last, don't take your being "Asian" and your girlfriend being "Asian" for granted; work at communication and at making first, second, and third impressions in as arduous and consistent a manner as a non-Asian guy would with your girl. Work just as hard at impressing her parents. They're not going to like you just because you're Asian. If anything, they'll expect more." King, age 34, NY.

I am gathering more material for a book that will expand on this chapter and it will include how Asian males feel about Asian females. The book will also deal with Asian males dating and marrying Asian females not of their own ethnicities (such as a Chinese guy marrying a Japanese woman) and non-Asian women. If anyone is interested in contributing a story to this book, please email me at Ming@AsianSocials.com. Most of the other advice in this book applies to Asian men as well as other men, so read on for more details on how to attract Asian women!

PART 2

ASIAN CULTURE

CHAPTER 7

ABOUT ASIANS

WHO ARE ASIANS?

Asians include: Chinese; Filipino; Japanese; Asian Indian; Korean; Vietnamese; Laotian; Thai; Cambodian; Pakistani; Indonesian and Hmong.

Pacific Islanders include: Polynesian (Hawaiian, Samoan, and Tongan); Micronesian (Guamanian) and Melanesian (Fijian).

The Asian culture section will focus on Chinese, Filipino, Japanese, Korean, Vietnamese, and Thai because these are the Asians most frequently encountered in the United States.

Do not refer to Asians as "Orientals." Many Asians take offense when people call them Orientals, which conveys images of colonialism and the exotic Orient. The word "Oriental" has connotations to objects such as rugs; Asians are people.

The population of Asian and Pacific Islanders in the United States was 1.5 million in 1970, 3.5 million in 1980, 7.3 million in 1990, 9.6 million in 1996, and approximately 10.2 million in February 1998, comprising 3.8 percent of the total U.S. population. According to the most recent U.S. Census data (March 2000,

Internet release date June 28, 2001, http://www.census.gov/population/socdemo/race/api/ppl-146/tab01.txt), the number of Asian and Pacific Islanders in the U.S. now totals over 10 million. Asian females constitute about 51 percent of the total U.S. Asian population.

Asian Americans differ in language, culture (food, customs, clothing, music, and so on), and time of immigration into the United States. However, there are certain attitudes toward family, respect, and relationships that many Asians have in common.

The Chinese and Japanese have been in the United States for generations. Pacific Islanders have populated the United States for over a century. Only a small number of Pacific Islanders are foreign-born. Immigration is the main reason for the growth of the Asian and Pacific Islander population, with many Asians coming to the United States after the enactment of the Immigration Act of 1965.

In the most recent census estimate, the median age of the Asian female population was 30.5, with the 25-34 age group being the most populous.

According to the U.S. Census, White husband/Asian wife couples are the most common interracial couples in the United States. (See Race of Wife by Race of Husband, "http://www.census.gov/population/socdemo/race/interractab1.txt" http://www.census.gov/population/socdemo/race/interractab1.txt. See also CaucAsia Links, Statistics and Studies, http://members.tripod.com/~scipoet/asianlinks.html.) Also, according to the *Washington Post*, 45 percent of U.S.-born Asian Pacific American women marry white men. (See "Interracial Marriages Eroding Barriers", by Michael A. Fletcher, December 28, 1998, http://www.washingtonpost.com/wp-srv/national/daily/dec98/melt29.htm.)

The majority of the Asian population lives in just six states in the United States (Source: Census 2000):

California (3,697,513 Asians, or 10.9% of the CA resident population)
New York (1,044,976 Asians, or 5% of the NY resident population)
Hawaii (503,868 Asians, or over 50% of the HI resident population, including native Hawaiians and other Pacific Islanders)
Texas (562,319 Asians, or 2.7% of the TX resident population)
New Jersey (480,276 Asians, or 5.7% of the NJ resident population)
Illinois (423,603 Asians, or 3.4% of the IL resident population)

MING'S HINT: If you want to increase your chances of meeting Asian friends, visit these states.

Asian and Pacific Islander women are *least* likely to be unemployed than any other group of women. (The unemployment rate of Asian women at 4.4 percent in March 1996 was lower than the national average for all women and was lower than that for any other individual group of women— 10.2 percent of Hispanic women were unemployed; African-American women, 10.0 percent; and white women, 4.7 percent).

The highest numbers of Asian and Pacific Islander women are employed in the technical, sales, and administrative support sector, the most populated sector for all other female racial groups as well. The Asian female occupational distribution is similar to white women's in managerial/professional specialty and service jobs. Due to the high educational attainment of Asian and Pacific Islander women, they have a high probability of getting jobs in management and professional careers. The employment statistics for Asian women in technical, sales, administrative support and operator, fabricator, and laborer positions are similar to statistics for African-American women.

Asian and Pacific Islander women have the highest median income of all female groups. This is perhaps due to their high educational attainment. Education is strongly valued in Asian communities.

Many Asian and Pacific Islanders have arrived in America to pursue American higher education; thus, you can find a lot of Asian females in colleges and graduate schools. Educational attainment varies by Asian group; Japanese, Chinese, Koreans, Indians and Hawaiians are the most highly educated among Asians.

There are over 5.6 million Asian females in the United States and over 1.5 million of them are single and of marriageable age.

For more information about Asians from the U.S. Census Bureau, go to http://www.census.gov/prod/2000pubs/p20-529.pdf.

ASIANS AND INTERNET USAGE

According to *Asian-Americans and the Internet*, a study done by the Pew Internet & American Life Project, 75% of English-speaking Asian-Americans use the Internet. Asian-Americans use the Internet on a daily basis and for longer hours than any other group in the U.S. Asian-American women prefer to do fun things on the Net such as downloading music, discovering information about fun activities, and shopping. This study leads me to believe that many Asian men and women also go on dating sites to meet potential dates. For example, many of the ladies I surveyed for this book had posted their profiles on the Internet. Also, many of my Asian female friends and I spend several hours a day chatting, surfing and posting messages on the Internet. For the entire report about Asian-Americans and the Internet, go to http://www.pewinternet.org/reports/toc.asp?Report=52.

ASIANS AND MONEY

The Chinese in America are very enthusiastic about stock investing; Charles Schwab and TD Waterhouse even opened up special branches in New York's Chinatown. The Asian stock markets are much riskier than the American stock market, and the Chinese have a high tolerance for risk. According to the previously cited study done by Pewinternet.org, Asian-Americans are four times as likely to purchase and sell stocks online than whites on any given day.

A study done on the Chinese and Vietnamese in California showed that most Chinese and Vietnamese pay off the entire balance of their credit cards every month.

ASIANS AND GROCERY SHOPPING

Asians not only shop in American grocery stores, but also shop in Asian grocery stores for ingredients not available elsewhere. A study done in California showed that around 63% of Chinese and Vietnamese surveyed shop at an Asian supermarket at least once a week. Food is very important to Asians. Many Asians only feel well if they have rice with every meal. However, this is definitely not true for every Asian-American. For Asians who have moved to the United States relatively late in their lives it might be true; but for Americanized Asian-Americans, I don't think they have a "preference" for Asian food at meals. Rather, they do need Asian food, but only as part of a very diverse American diet that includes food from every ethnic culture.

BOBO TEAS

The *New York Times* recently printed an article about *bobo* drinks, which are flavored teas with chewy tapioca pearls. A lot of Asians, particularly Chinese, love these drinks, and lounge around in teahouses all over the United States drinking *bobo* tea while socializing with friends. Find a *bobo* teahouse and you will find Asians.

SALTY PLUMS (*MEI*)

Many Asians love salty plums, which are preserved, salted and sour plums that taste so intense, your mouth waters just thinking about them. Salty plums taste a bit like olives, but are sweeter and more flavorful. Also, there are Chinese preserved olives, which are dried, sweet and salty. If you are ever in Chinatown in New York, look for a store called *Aji Ichiban*, which sells about 30 varieties of salty plums—in addition to dried squid, Japanese crackers, and candies.

They offer samples of almost everything they sell, so you can taste before you buy. Plum is one of the favorite flavors of Asian soft drinks, tea, ice cream, candy, and so on. Every Asian market sells salty plums because it is the one of the most popular snacks for many Asians.

ASIANS AND LONG DISTANCE PHONE CALLS

Many Asians tend to spend over $100 every month calling family members in Asia. International phone cards are also popular.

THE ASIAN VOTE

Asians tend to vote Democrat. According to the *Los Angles Times* national exit poll, Gore received 62% of all Asian votes while Bush received 37%. The results all over the nation for Asians were similar. Prior to 1992, however, the Asian vote was largely Republican.

ASIAN MEDIA STARS

The website of *Entertainment Weekly* recommended that if you want to be a successful actor or actress, then you should take up martial arts like Kelly Hu, the Asian actress in *The Scorpion King*. Why do so many Asian movie stars know martial arts? Perhaps this is because martial arts is a popular form of Asian culture; however, many actors complain that there are very few roles for Asian actors out there due to stereotyping. Michelle Yeoh reported that Hollywood had trouble explaining an Asian face in films when she tried to break into American films in 1995, despite the fact that she was one of the most popular and highest paid actresses in Asia. As you know, Michelle Yeoh became famous in the U.S. for her action parts in *Tomorrow Never Dies* and *Crouching Tiger, Hidden Dragon*. Many complain that Hollywood still has difficulty casting Asian women as "normal" people who don't know any martial arts. Some signs that this is changing include shows such as *Ally McBeal*, *Arliss*, and *The View*, which feature Asians as "normal" people.

CHAPTER 8

The Various Asian Cultures

Non-Asians have asked many Asians insulting questions about the differences between Chinese, Japanese, or some other Asian ethnicities. Some Asians are also unsure of the backgrounds of other Asians. However, there are certain clues that can clue you into the background of an Asian person. The one most important thing you need to do to distinguish between different Asians is to get at least a superficial familiarity with the different sounds of Asian languages; people who can speak and are familiar with Asian languages can tell whether someone is Chinese or Japanese in a second. How do you become familiar with Asian languages? Make friends with people of various Asian backgrounds and listen to them speak the different Asian languages. Note their accents. What makes Korean sound different from Chinese? Listen often and you will know. Some good places you can meet Asian friends are churches, Asian clubs and restaurants, and the international students centers that are in or close to your neighborhood. A good website for you to visit to familiarize yourself with various Asian cultures and people is VirtualTourist.com, a site that contains lots of cultural tips and postings from people who have traveled to various Asian countries. You have the opportunity there to contact people all over the world who are interested in travel and different cultures at VirtualTourist.com.

Another way to distinguish Asians from one another, especially if the Asians are Asian-Americans who speak English (without accents) and have either forgotten or never learned their parents' native tongues, is to look at their last names. Japanese last names are often polysyllabic, with three or four syllables, such as Kawasaki. Korean and Chinese last names are usually one syllable. A common Korean last name is Kim. Filipino last names often sound Spanish, due to the Spanish influence in the Philippines. To learn last names, you should simply see what are the most popular names and simply learn them, memorize them. It's not that hard. Note that there are names that are common to several ethnicities. For example, Lee is both a Korean and Chinese name. Some Hawaiian and Japanese names overlap because of the Japanese influence in Hawaii.

Some people claim they can tell Asians apart by their faces and body types. One Korean guy I know used to think he could but after being in Asia for a year and traveling to China, Thailand, Vietnam, Cambodia, Japan, and within Korea, he admits that there are definitely patterns and certain general rules and tendencies. None of these rules is more true that this one: exceptions always abound. There are Koreans who look Chinese, Japanese, Cambodian, as well as Chinese who look Hmong, Korean, and so on. The Japanese, Korean, Thai, etc. "Look" or "type" is a constructed look and type that has as many exceptions—if not more—as it does adherents.

It should be noted that the following descriptions of the various Asian cultures are generalities and there might be exceptions. Also, this chapter is not intended to be a crash course in Asian culture. Some women I've interviewed have reported that some men on the street have been insensitive enough to say to them: "I know you Asians" or something of a similar nature. If you take away one thing from this book, take away this advice: Do not say thoughtless, racially oriented things to strangers on the street, no matter how innocent and sweet they look.

There is no single, unifying, universal ASIAN culture just as there is no unifying universal WHITE culture. Each Asian culture is as unique and vibrant and rich as any individual world culture. Within this big thing we call WHITE culture, there is Italian, Irish, German, Swede, English, and French culture; just as non-Asian culture is diverse and has individual components that are related yet distinct, so are Asian cultures as unique and different as Italian, Irish, German, and so on. I am offering only broad brush strokes of each culture, and if someone really wants to learn an Asian culture he has to spend a lifetime doing so. Each culture is huge and not capable of being defined in a closed stereotyped way; for example, how accurate are European stereotypes of Americans? Some Asian cultures consider other Asian cultures to be as alien to them as a non-Asian culture. There are tensions among Asians themselves resulting from their history, e.g. Koreans and Chinese traditionally dislike the Japanese, Cambodians don't like Vietnamese, and so on. In the United States today, there is less tension between the different Asian ethnicities.

Once you understand the richness of each Asian culture and how "Asian" means many different things to many people, remember that for many Asian-Americans—the more Americanized ones—the following rules and etiquettes and cultural knowledge are not as applicable. One should always figure out an Asian lady's relation to her own Asian background—that is, see if she even has one—before bringing up anything "Asian". Only certain parts of the below criteria and cultural characteristics may apply to the Korean, Chinese, or Thai girl you are chasing!

One Asian female interviewee said:

> *"It is all individual as to what culture, background, childhood each person had. So there shouldn't be any differentiation by looks or attitude that tell what country they are from. To distinguish among us is to defeat the purpose of what we are trying to do all the time ....overcoming stereotypes." Alisa, age 30, CA.*

Asian Etiquette Tips

Why should you worry about Asian etiquette? You should learn the rules of etiquette because knowing them will help you attract an Asian woman. Good manners are very important in Asian cultures. Knowing the rules of etiquette will show that you care about Asian culture and behaving correctly. This will reflect positively in your Asian love interest's eyes. These rules apply to many Asians in general, no matter where they live. Therefore, follow them whether you want to impress an Asian girl living in Asia or in the United States. This is less true for very Americanized Asian-Americans.

The tips below are general "Asian" etiquette tips that don't apply to every Asian culture and in every Asian situation, but it is better to be safe than sorry!

Table Manners

- To show that you are polite, you should always pour and refill your guest's teacup before refilling yours.
- Never, ever stick your chopsticks straight up in the rice bowl, as this resembles burning incense to mourn the dead.
- Do not point your chopsticks at anyone.
- When your host says that her food is not good, do not agree with her. It is a form of politeness to put down one's own accomplishments, which is one of the basic principles most Asians are taught. Never agree with anyone when he or she puts down herself. You are supposed to disagree with her and tell her how great she is.
- Do not turn over fish when you are done with the top of the fish. Instead, carefully remove the bones with a utensil to get to the fish beneath the bones. It is considered bad luck to flip the fish over.
- Do not have the tail of the fish pointing to anyone, because whoever has the tail pointed at him or her will soon lose his or her job.
- Try not to drop your chopsticks as this is considered bad luck.

The Various Asian Cultures

It is also bad luck to cross over your chopsticks. However, at a dim sum restaurant, this is permissible to show that you are ready for the check.

Sushi Etiquette

Do not rub your chopsticks together to get rid of the splinters. This is insulting and implies that the restaurant or host does not provide you with proper utensils.

Dip the fish in soy sauce to flavor the fish. Do not dip it rice-side down because this will cause the rice to fall into the soy sauce.

Ginger is to be eaten to cleanse the palate between pieces of sushi.

Do not bite half of a piece of sushi and then put the other half down. Eat the entire piece of sushi after you have picked it up.

If you are picking food up from a shared plate, then use the clean side of the chopstick that has not touched your mouth.

Do not pick up a plate with the same hand that you are using to hold your chopsticks.

Eat all of your food. It is impolite to leave any food, especially rice.

Gifts

Give gifts from your own country of origin. If you are giving a gift to someone in or from China, do not give anything made in China. For example, if you are from the United States, try giving something that reflects American culture such as a book in English about whatever it is that your Asian girlfriend likes or perhaps a CD by a popular American artist. Some Asians are practical, so they prefer useful gifts over "frivolous" gifts. This may not apply to women who are more Americanized, so check with your girlfriend to find out what she prefers.

It is polite to refuse your gift many times before she accepts it, so make sure you offer it to her many times. She will refuse your gift to show that she is not greedy.

If you are giving an Asian woman something for her hair or head, make sure it is not white in color. This is because wearing white in the hair is a custom for Asian people in mourning.

In Japan it is unlucky to present items in even numbers (especially for weddings where it can symbolize divorce.) The idea is that even numbers are divisible by 2 and therefore not as "strong" as uneven numbers. In Japan and China, the number four (4) is unlucky because it sounds like "*shi*" or death in both Mandarin Chinese and Japanese. Also, in Japan, the number nine (9) is considered unlucky as well, because it is pronounced "*ku*," which sounds like agony or anguish in Japanese and Chinese. Also, for Chinese New Year, it is good luck to bring three (3) Mandarin oranges to a Chinese home because the oranges signify gold. Do not bring four (4) oranges, because four means death! The numbers 88 or 888 are also lucky numbers in Chinese culture, because the number eight (8), pronounced "*ba*" sounds like "*fa*," or wealth in Chinese. The number six (6) ("*liu*") is considered lucky by the Chinese because it sounds like a carefree life. The number nine (9) ("*jiu*") is also lucky because it sounds like eternity in Chinese, and September 9 is a very lucky wedding day for eternal marriage.

When wrapping your gift, use red or gold wrapping, as they are symbols of good luck. Do not use black or white because they signify death.

Things not to give:

Knives or scissors: These are signs of severing a relationship.

White or yellow flowers: Certain flowers are for visiting someone in a hospital or mourning the dead. Although this rule against flowers is not followed strictly these days, your choice in flowers should not include chrysanthemums, as they are often for funerals.

Clocks: The word for clock sounds like "attending a funeral" in Cantonese and some Chinese consider it bad luck to receive a clock.

Meeting An Asian Woman's Family

Depending on your Asian girlfriend, you may or may not be invited to meet her family soon after dating her. Some Asian families are stricter than others, and may oppose the dating of a non-Asian. Also, some families have a rule of not meeting boyfriends until the relationship is serious. If you are invited to meet an Asian woman's family, you are moving forward in a relationship with her and you should be flattered.

Often, Asians prefer to entertain in restaurants because their homes may not be large enough to entertain guests. However, this may not be true in your case. Talk with your Asian girlfriend to find out about her family's preferences.

When you meet an Asian woman's family, you should bring a small, appropriate gift. Reread the Asian Etiquette section to decide what to give and what not to give. Ask your girlfriend for tips as well. For example, do not give scissors or other cutting tools or clocks. Food is always appropriate, as it is practical and preferred by Asians. Wrap the gifts in red for good luck, and expect your host to refuse the gift a few times to be polite.

CHINESE CULTURE

Chinese people are from a number of different areas: Taiwan (Republic of China), Mainland China (People's Republic of China), Hong Kong, Singapore, and other countries. People in Taiwan and Mainland China speak Mandarin, the standard Chinese language taught in schools. Mainland Chinese often end their words with the sound "er." The dialect spoken in Hong Kong is Cantonese, which is completely different from Mandarin. While people in Mainland China are somewhat more practical, people in Hong Kong and Singapore indulge more often in luxury, brand-name goods.

The following are some of the more traditional Chinese values. Depending on how Westernized your Chinese girlfriend is, the following cultural characteristics may or may not apply to her. However, it is good to be aware of these attitudes and traditions.

In Chinese culture, family approval is important, so be sure to be nice to your Chinese lady's parents in order to have a smooth relationship with her. It is polite to learn a few phrases in Chinese to show that you appreciate Chinese culture. Note that you should use these phrases after you get to know the lady and not as pick-up lines. It is the view of more traditional Chinese parents that Western men are not sincere about marriage and family, so try to show that you are serious.

Most Western cultures do not place as bad a stigma on divorce as the Chinese. Many Chinese women who are divorced or widowed have a hard time finding Chinese men to date or marry. Such ladies prefer American men, who are more understanding of their situation.

Many Chinese have adverse reactions to alcohol, so keep this in mind when you ask them out for drinks. Perhaps a better suggestion would be tea or coffee.

Chinese art includes pottery and porcelain; cloisonné (applying colorful enamel to the surface of copper or bronze); calligraphy; embroidery; traditional Chinese painting; Chinese dance and Chinese opera.

Chinese Names

In a Chinese name, the last name is always first. For example, if a woman is named Wang Mei Li, then her last name is Wang and her first name is Mei Li. If her name is Wang Mei, her last name is Wang, and her first name is Mei. Formally, she should be addressed as Miss Wang. Informally, you should call her by her full name, i.e. Wang Mei or Wang Mei Li.

A married Chinese woman keeps her maiden name, but the kids take the father's last name.

Chinese people who do business or interact with Western people take on Western first names and put their last names behind their first names, i.e. Jackie Chan, Connie Chung, Lucy Liu.

It is common for a Chinese person not to have a religion. Instead, Chinese values are influenced by the teachings of Confucius, which put high importance on four basic virtues: loyalty, respect for parents and elders, benevolence, and righteousness.

Confucius also promoted the following rules in relationships:

Husband and Wife: A wife is to obey her husband and the husband must support his wife.
Parent and Child: Children should never disobey their fathers, and parents need to provide for and educate their children. Children must respect their parents and take care of them in their old age.
Older and younger: The older a person, the wiser he or she is, and therefore, one's elders are to be respected and obeyed.
Between friends: Friends need to be loyal to each other.
Ruler and subjects: Rulers must do everything to better the lives of their subjects and the subjects must be faithful to their rulers.

Keep the foregoing rules in mind when you observe a Chinese lady's actions and decisions, and if at all possible, try to be respectful to elders in front of her. This is showing respect for her culture and she will appreciate it. If your Chinese lady is Americanized, however, she will probably not believe that the wife needs to obey the husband.

Use both hands when offering anything, such as a business card or gift, to your Chinese lady to show respect.

Turn your chopstick around when serving food to others. This is because the other side is not contaminated with your saliva.

Chinese people love it when someone non-Chinese attempts to speak to them in their own language, so try to learn some Chinese phrases. However, Chinese phrases are risky pick-up lines because not all Asian women are Chinese. You might offend the lady if she is not Chinese because she will think that you think all Asians look alike. It is best to wait until you've known a Chinese lady for a few days before you try some Chinese phrases on her.

CHINESE-AMERICANS

The vast majority of Chinese-Americans reside either in California or the New York Metropolitan area. Most (around 75%) Chinese-Americans are foreign-born. However, since Chinese-Americans tend to be very well educated, most of them, except for the most recent immigrants, speak English and have assimilated into American society.

The largest group of Asians in the United States is Chinese-American. Many Chinese-Americans are conservative in both their personal lives and business and tend to plan for the future. The most widely read Chinese language newspaper is the *World Journal*, with a large circulation in Atlanta, Boston, Chicago, Florida, Hawaii, Los Angeles, Texas, New York, Philadelphia, Washington, D.C., San Francisco and Seattle. The above-listed cities and states are where the majority of Chinese-Americans reside. You would do well to go and get a copy of the *World Journal* and look for ads for places Chinese-Americans visit for entertainment and for parties advertised in the personals section ("*Hun You*" section) of the paper. Chinese women also often place personals ads in the *World Journal*. They are interested in meeting both Asian and non-Asian men. Make it easy for them to find you; advertise in the *World Journal*. Lots of Asian singles read the *World Journal*, so you might want to put a personals ad in the personals section if you are serious about getting a Chinese girlfriend. The *World Journal* will translate your ad into Chinese for you, or you can place an ad in English. The good thing about an English ad in a Chinese newspaper is that you will probably get responses only from women who can read English (unless the ladies get the ad translated). However, for more responses place an ad in Chinese.

I place ads in the *World Journal* inviting everyone to my AsianSocials.com parties and get enthusiastic responses from Chinese ladies. I had the opportunity to speak to quite a few of the Chinese ladies who responded to my ads, and was quite surprised that many of them wanted to meet "American" (non-Asian) men. My research has revealed to me that many Chinese-American ladies would like to date non-Asians. Some of these ladies have kids and suspect that Asian men would not accept their kids. However, many other Asian ladies I spoke to preferred Asian men because they felt more comfortable with them. Most of the women who responded to my ad were educated, English-speaking, and well-settled in the United States. The following table indicates that the *World Journal* is available in many major cities in the United States, so it would be worth your while to place an ad in this popular paper.

WORLD JOURNAL

EDITION	CIRCULATION
Atlanta	5,000
Boston	10,000
Chicago	12,000
Florida	6,000
Hawaii	5,500
Los Angeles/Texas	100,000
New York	80,000
Philadelphia/Washington D.C.	12,000
San Francisco/Seattle	68,000
Total	298,500

LOS ANGELES
1588 Corporate Center Drive
Monterey, CA 91754
Tel. (213) 268-4982
Fax. (213) 265-3476

NEW YORK
141-07 20th Avenue
Whitestone, NY 11357
Tel. (718) 746-8889
Fax. (718) 746-5972

SAN FRANCISCO
231 Adrian Road
Millbrae, CA 94030
Tel. (415) 692-9936
Fax. (415) 692-8665

Visiting a Chinese Home

When you are invited to visit a Chinese home, you will almost always be treated to a meal. The Chinese do not feel like they are proper hosts unless there is a sumptuous meal involved in the visit.

Bring a gift with you when you visit. Try to give something useful, such as a fruit basket or chocolates. Avoid giving flowers, as some Chinese associate flowers with funerals. Wrap the gift in red. Your host might refuse it several times before finally accepting it to be polite.

Most likely, the mother of the household will be doing the cooking and will cook one course at a time in the kitchen. Thus, she might not be eating with you. You should ask if the mother will be joining your meal and then proceed to eat and not wait for her. She will likely put down her own cooking, and your reaction should be one of lavish praise for the food. You will notice that the Chinese like to put themselves down, and you should contradict every putdown with compliments.

Recommended Reading List for Understanding Chinese Culture:

Passport Taiwan: Your Pocket Guide to Taiwanese Business, Customs & Etiquette (Passport to the World)
By Jeffrey E. Curry, Barbara Szerlip
Paperback - 96 pages (October 1997) World Trade Press; ISBN: 1885073275; Dimensions (in inches): 4.25 x 6.99 x 4.25

Bound Feet & Western Dress
Pang-Mei Natasha Chang
Paperback - 215 pages Reprint edition (October 1997) Anchor Books; ISBN: 0385479646; Dimensions (in inches): 0.62 x 8.01 x 5.22

Chinese Business Etiquette: A Guide to Protocol, Manners, and Culture in the People's Republic of China
Paperback - 304 pages (March 1999) Warner Books; ISBN: 0446673870; Dimensions (in inches): 0.86 x 8.09 x 5.35
This is an excellent book to find out more about the psychology of the Chinese, written by someone who has lived and done business in China.

List of websites for Chinese-American groups, events and culture: http://directory.google.com/Top/Society/Ethnicity/Asian/Asian-American/Chinese_American/

JAPANESE CULTURE

African-American culture is very popular in Japan, and the youth of Japan are celebrating African-American culture by sporting dreadlocks and tans. Many Japanese women love African-American men, so if you are an African-American man, you will probably be very appreciated by these women! Furthermore, Japanese celebrate American culture, fashion and music.

Here are some more Japanese culture tidbits from the point of view of a Japanese-American female in New York:

- Hair dying is very popular with Japanese girls (especially those who come from Japan). Very few I know or see in New York City keep their natural hair color.
- I also tend to see more first generation Japanese here in New York than I do in places out West like California.
- Japanese (perhaps Asian in general) tend to put others first so as not to appear rude. For example, when dining with a group, it is not polite to take the best piece of meat or exhibit otherwise "greedy" or "selfish" mannerisms.
- It is seen as impolite to be overly boisterous (such as laughing loudly, unnecessarily drawing attention to yourself, and so on).

Traditional Japanese art includes: flower arrangement; tea

ceremony; kimono dressing; origami; calligraphy and clay art. There is a rich modern artistic tradition in Japan, more so, than in other Asian countries because of how Westernized Japan has become in comparison to other Asian nations. It has a rich film industry and a rich modern literature, for example. Japanese, as a result of early Westernization and modernization, tend to also more openly accept non-Asian values, cultures, and men.

Around 75% of Japanese people believe that blood types influence the personality of a person. Often, Japanese people reveal their blood types to casual acquaintances to get to know each other better.

Type A: peaceful, serious, quiet

Type B: high-energy and enthusiastic

Type AB: sensitive, careful, and sentimental

Type O: harmonious, friendly, gregarious, and opinionated

Comment by a Caucasian male:

> *"One thing I've observed about Japanese is a strong sense of "purity" and "impurity." The feet and the ground are considered to be of a lower vibration and so it's imperative to avoid dropping certain things on the ground or to have the feet touch certain things.*
>
> *This sense of purity also applies to the spreading of germs. It is common in Japan for people with colds to wear surgical masks to prevent their germs from spreading. Some Japanese in the U.S., even those under the age of 30, also have this habit, though it appears many of them abandon this practice out of fear of standing out too much. Certainly, you need not don a mask yourself, but I would be a bit more diligent than usual with the hygiene rules your mother taught you as a kid—even if you haven't caught any bug."*
> *Ted, age 35, WA.*

JAPANESE-AMERICANS

Japanese-Americans are the only Asians that are largely second and third generation Americans. This is due to the small number of Japanese who have immigrated to the US since World War II. Most Japanese-Americans immigrated into the US around 1902. The Japanese were discouraged from immigrating into the US due to political circumstances during WWII and the economic boom in Japan in the late 1980s.

Some Japanese-American cultural characteristics include the preference of name brands and the emphasis placed on the value of popular opinion over individual opinion.

The majority of Japanese-Americans live in the following states: California, Hawaii, New York, Washington, Illinois, New Jersey, Texas, Oregon, Colorado, and Michigan.

SOME OF THE MORE TRADITIONAL JAPANESE VALUES INCLUDE:

The Japanese value surface harmony and avoid open confrontation. To avoid hurt feelings, the Japanese will sometimes not say "no" directly and bluntly.

Japanese people are more implicit and expect you to read their actions. Unlike American society, where people say things as explicitly as possible, the most important points of conversations in Japanese society are often left unspoken. You need to look for subtle hints.

Like Chinese values, Japanese values are influenced by the teachings of Confucius, which put high importance on four basic virtues: loyalty, respect for parents and elders, benevolence, and righteousness. Keep this in mind when you observe an Asian female's actions and decisions; if at all possible, try to be respectful to elders in front of her. This is showing respect for her culture and she will appreciate it. Keep in mind, however, that the more Americanized Japanese women may not agree that the wife must obey her husband.

Gift Giving

Gifts are important to the Japanese; therefore, you must be thoughtful in your gifts. The Japanese consider gifts to come from the heart and convey feelings better than words. (The Japanese word "*kokoro*" denotes this ineffable reservoir of feelings and heart for the Japanese.) To show respect, present your gift with both hands, and say something humble about your gift, such as "This is something of little value." Gifts are often not opened in front of the giver; so don't be surprised if your lady does not open it. When your lady gives you a gift, remember to thank her several times, even the next time you see her. It is impolite to arrive as a guest at someone's home without bringing a gift. Gifts are often given when just meeting others for the first time.

Do not give the following:

Any cutting utensils, such as knives, scissors, or letter openers, as they symbolize the severing of relationships.
White handkerchiefs, which symbolize mourning.
Anything in the numbers of four and nine, as these numbers are unlucky.
White and yellow chrysanthemums, as they are for funerals.

Giving Compliments

The Japanese will react to a compliment by saying something humble that puts themselves down. To receive a compliment wholeheartedly would appear too vain. The Japanese value modesty.

The Meaning of *Hai*

"*Hai*" is yes in Japanese, and Japanese etiquette often requires the listener to say yes during a conversation. If your lady says yes while she is conversing with you, it may not mean that she is agreeing with you, only that she is listening to you. Therefore, it is important to listen carefully to what your Japanese girlfriend is saying in the full context of the conversation.

The Importance of Respect

It is very important to respect your Japanese lady's culture, and not put down anything she does. The Japanese care a lot about not "losing face." "Losing face" means being humiliated or embarrassed in front of others. Therefore, try to learn as much as you can about Japanese culture, and try to participate in some traditional and modern Japanese cultural activities, if you can.

To Learn More About Japanese Culture, go to:

http://evilkrisii.tripod.com/index2.html
> EvilKris is an English guy who is extremely funny and knows a lot about the Japanese. His website contains reviews of books you should read to find out more about Japanese culture and how to "survive like a bastard" in Japan.

To meet Japanese friends, go to Http://www.HappyGold.com, where you can post messages for Japanese ePals for cultural, language and social exchange.

Visiting a Japanese Home

You should remove your overcoat, hat, gloves and shoes prior to entering a Japanese home. Take care that you do not have any holes in your socks, as this is not proper. Bring a present of food that is wrapped beautifully, as the Japanese view packaging and presentation as very important.

Japanese Reading List:

Japanese Business Etiquette: A Practical Guide to Success with the Japanese
By Diana Rowland
Updated and Revised Second Edition
Paperback, ISBN: 0-446-39518-8
Excellent book about Japanese culture. Very useful if you want to understand the Japanese.

Japanese at a Glance: Phrase Book and Dictionary
By Nobuo Akiyama, Carol Akiyama
Paperback 3rd pocket edition (May 1998) Barrons Educational Series; ISBN: 0764103202; Dimensions (in inches): 0.82 x 6.20 x 3.87
This book can be very useful in your communications with Japanese friends. Beginning with an easy to understand pronunciation guide, the book lists thousands of practical phrases in a multitude of contexts in everyday life.
The book also includes Japanese-English, English-Japanese glossary, and brief explanations of the Japanese writing system and grammar.

The Japanese Today: Change and Continuity
By Edwin O. Reischauer, et al
Paperback - 459 pages (March 1995) Harvard Univ Pr; ISBN: 0674471849; Dimensions (in inches): 1.07 x 9.17 x 6.33

Understanding Japanese Society
By Joy Hendry
Paperback - 240 pages 2nd edition (April 1995) Routledge; ISBN: 0415102596; Dimensions (in inches): 0.60 x 8.42 x 5.43

Making Out in Japanese
By Todd and Erika Geers
Paperback - 104 pages Reprint edition (May 1988) Charles E

The Various Asian Cultures

Tuttle Co; ISBN: 4900737097 ; Dimensions (in inches): 0.34 x 7.19 x 4.36

Audio Cassette (December 1988) Charles E Tuttle Co; ISBN: 0804817138

These items are available used on Amazon.com.

Some people say this book contains outdated Japanese, but the Japanese phrases are good for entertainment purposes at least.

Outrageous Japanese: Slang, Curses and Epithets
Paperback (May 1992) Charles E Tuttle Co; ISBN: 0804816948 ; Dimensions (in inches): 0.36 x 7.18 x 4.35

Contains insults, curses and body part words in Japanese. Some Japanese speakers find this funny.

KOREAN CULTURE

Koreans, like most other Asians, are influenced by the teachings of Confucius, which emphasize loyalty, respect for parents and elders, benevolence, and righteousness.

Education is the way to increase one's social status and style of life for many Koreans. Koreans are among the most—if not *the* most—obsessed and successful at American education. Numerous Koreans are enrolled in the nation's elite colleges and graduate schools, and working at top companies.

Do not leave your chopsticks sticking straight up in a bowl of rice, which looks like the incense burned to memorialize the dead during Korean neo-Confucian ancestral rites carried out several times a year. This is true for Japanese and Chinese as well – the image is associated with the symbolic act of feeding the dead during special ceremonies.

It is polite to refuse food and gifts twice before finally accepting, so as to not appear too greedy. Therefore, if you are offering food or gifts to a Korean, offer it a few times if she objects.

The majority of Korean-Americans reside in the following states:

California, New York, Illinois, New Jersey, Texas, Maryland, Virginia, Washington, Pennsylvania and Hawaii.

Here is what one Korean-American male said about Korean culture:

> *"Koreans are, in my opinion, one of the more fiery Asian races. They tend to get quite passionate in arguments and fights; the stereotype of the quiet, passive Asian applies the least to Koreans.*
>
> *Modesty is not something as valued in Korean society as it is in Japanese society, for instance; Koreans tend to be a little more boastful. A recent survey by CNN among Korean males, for instance, found that young Korean males—more than other Asian males—were more sexually confident and experienced than young men of other Asian nationalities.*
>
> *Koreans are very proud of distinct cultural achievements such as Hangeul (the phonetic alphabet the Korean dynasty king Sejong made in his efforts to make the masses literate), celadon porcelain (world-famous), and other traditional Korean musics and arts.*
>
> *Koreans also tend to be very direct and frank about body weight, age, physical appearance, salary, and other matters considered private and personal by most Americans. Therefore, one shouldn't be immediately turned off by a line of questioning from a Korean female that might seem interrogative and intrusive; these are standard Korean dating questions.*
>
> *Family is very important for Koreans. Children are supported by their parents at least through their university years; in turn, many children support their aging parents. It is common practice for eldest sons to hand their first paycheck to their parents.*

There is a very recent and painful history Koreans share with Japanese due to the latter's colonization of Korea from the turn of the century till the end of World War II. Do not take a Korean for a Japanese or confuse the two nations. The Korean will be deeply offended.

Although Koreans tend to be more direct, frank, haughty, and even more rude than Japanese and Chinese, respect still plays an important role in society and is a very important value. Nowhere is this more reflected than in the Korean vernacular language of Hangeul: Koreans, even young Koreans, have many terms that they use to refer to people in various social relations with them. Different terms are used for women and men, younger and older people. Only towards friends and younger people does one call people by their first names. Also, there are different levels of formality in the language: among friends and younger persons, one uses "ban mal"; to elders and persons of higher station, one uses higher forms for the verb endings of every Korean sentence.

About Korean drinking culture: This is very big in Korea, bigger, I think, than it is in Japan and China. Drinking is an essential part of Korean social life. While drinking, reciprocity is very important; one pours for and receives the empty cups of one's drinking companions. One pours for one's elders. One must pour and receive with two hands. If one finishes one's cup, one is not allowed to refill his or her own cup; he must wait for someone to notice and fill it for him or her. If one is to meet a Korean girl's parents, especially her father, familiarity with Korean drinking customs would go a long way!

When receiving and giving gifts, always do it with both hands. (Koreans receive and give things, anything, with both hands when the exchange is with someone older and/or respected.)

As for religion: many Koreans are religious; Up to 40% of Koreans are Christian (mostly Protestant), 40%

Buddhist, and the other 20% a miscellaneous mix. Most Koreans in the U.S. are Christian; if one has a Christian background, this can only work to one's advantage when dating a Korean girl, I think.

Korean girls, more than Japanese (I'm not so sure about Chinese) are less apt to date and marry non-Koreans. Especially Korean females who've immigrated recently. Koreans tend also to be very nationalistic and so it will be quite a challenge, I think, for a non-Asian man to date a Korean lady. Much of this stems from the fact that Korea opened up to the West relatively recently, in comparison to other Asian countries. It's a very homogeneous nation. Foreigners are not totally welcome in all-modern Seoul, even, in comparison to Beijing and Tokyo. A foreign army still divides the country in half. Koreans are a small, tightly-knit group with lots of cultural and ethnic pride.

Korean dating is a bit on the conservative side. People are often introduced to each other by mutual acquaintances. There are special introduction meetings that happen to facilitate the meeting of new people. Mutual friends will actually go with a friend and another party, speak to both about their possibly dating each other, and then leave if things are going well. Thus, meeting Korean women—the less Americanized ones—will prove very difficult. And dangerous, since Korean men will tend to be around them as Koreans tend to hang out in big groups.

Korean arts include calligraphy, painting, pottery, literature, and many folk arts and music including pansori, drumming, fan dances, and music on a variety of Korean instruments." King, NY.

A Caucasian male who had lived in Korea for many years and who speaks fluent Korean, said that he did not date any women while he was in Korea because the Korean women he met refused to date foreigners. However, like King said in his quote above, this reluctance of Korean women to date non-Korean men applies to less Americanized Korean women, and might not apply to the Korean-American woman you are interested in.

Visiting a Korean Home

As with many Asian households, it is proper to bring a little gift when you are visiting. Nicely wrapped food gift items are great. Fruits are usually given when one visits someone else's house; when one is to get engaged to a Korean woman, elaborate sets of Korean rice-cakes are brought to the home of the woman's parents. Make sure you compliment the hostess for her hospitality. You might notice that other people will slurp their noodles; this is considered proper table manners and is often done to show one's enjoyment of the noodles.

Be prepared for some spicy food—non-Asian should know *kimchi* (spicy, fermented cabbage and other pickles)—and for some drinking with the father, most likely. Also the Korean wife usually does the cooking and presenting; the father, like most Asian father figures, does nothing in the home. Non-Asian men should not be put off if they drink only with the father and the mother is hardly visible; this is a feature of a more conservative Korean household.

Also, in Korean households—as in many Asian households—one must take off one's shoes before entering. This is very important! Not just a cultural thing, it's also considered sanitary. Koreans freak out if you walk around their house with your shoes on.

Reading List for Understanding Korean Culture

East to America: Korean American Life Stories
   By Elaine H. Kim

Still Life with Rice: A Young American Woman Discovers the Life and Legacy of Her Korean Grandmother
   By Hellie Lee

Korea Old and New: A History
   By Carter J. Eckert, Ki-Baik Lee

Passport Korea: Your Pocket Guide to Korean Business and Etiquette
   By Kevin Keating, Barbara Szerlip
   Paperback - 96 pages (October 1997) World Trade Press; ISBN: 1885073399; Dimensions (in inches): 0.27 x 7.00 x 4.25
   This is a good brief book about Korean culture.

Lonely Planet Korean Phrase Book
   By Young Ok Kim, et al
   Paperback - 208 pages 2nd edition (June 1995) Lonely Planet; ISBN: 0864423020; Dimensions (in inches): 0.49 x 4.99 x 3.63
   Good grammar and phrase book.

Native Speaker
   by Chang-Rae Lee
   This book is from a Korean-American male's point of view. A Korean-American male friend of mine considers it to be the first important novel to come from a Korean-American novelist that has been embraced by the American literary community. Many Korean-Americans identify with it as the first book to articulate their own lives and identity crises.

Vietnamese Culture

The majority of Vietnamese are Buddhists, but not all of them actively practice Buddhism. Vietnamese culture is also influenced by Confucianism and Taoism (which advocates the belief in harmony between man and nature).

Vietnamese-Americans

In the United States, the Vietnamese-American population represents approximately 8.9% of the Asian population, making the Vietnamese the 6th largest Asian population in the United States. Vietnamese reside in major metropolitan areas such as California, Texas, Florida, Louisiana, Virginia, Washington, New York, Massachusetts and Illinois.

RECOMMENDED READING LIST FOR VIETNAMESE CULTURE:

Lonely Planet Vietnam
Mason Florence, Robert Storey
Paperback - 616 pages 6th edition (March 2001) Lonely Planet; ISBN: 1864501898; Dimensions (in inches): 1.03 x 7.20 x 5.12

Lonely Planet Vietnamese Phrase Book
Thinh Hoang, et al
Paperback 3 edition (July 2000) Lonely Planet; ISBN: 0864426615; Dimensions (in inches): 0.65 x 5.49 x 3.64

Passport Vietnam: Your Pocket Guide to Vietnamese Business, Customs & Etiquette (Passport to the World) by Jeffrey E. Curry, Molly Thurmond, Chinh T. Nguyen

FILIPINO CULTURE

The Philippines is an archipelago of over 7,000 islands, inhabited by people of Malayan, Hispanic and American descent. The Filipina beauty is a mixture of these races. Filipinas look Asian with a bit of Spanish mixed in, often with tanned skin and straight black hair.

One Asian female reader wrote:

> *"I personally think that Vietnamese and Filipino women put on more make-up than Chinese women. Their skin is a bit darker and most of their hair is dyed brownish-yellowish." Jan, age 25, CT.*

A Caucasian male reader wrote:

> *"I have been all over Asia as a military man and as a result have become very attracted to Asian women and cultures. Most of all, I really became attracted to Filipina women. Filipinas are more Westernized than other Asian women and they speak English fluently. Filipinas are very friendly and loving and have good family values and exotic beauty. In general, most Asian women are very exotic with their petite bodies and sexy long silky hair."* Jack, age 32, PA.

FILIPINO CULTURE

For a list of 155 Filipino cultural characteristics, go to http://www.virtualtourist.com/.100547/article/87/13/?s=L&xxxxxxxxxxxx. (if this link is too long for you to type, just type in www.VirtualTourist.com, and go to the Philippines section and look under Cultural Tips.

Here is the real deal, guys, about how to impress a Filipina, straight from a lovely Filipina American herself:

1. **WHAT MAKES A FILIPINA DIFFERENT FROM OTHER WOMEN?**
   I can sum it all up in three traits:
- **Sensitive and emotional** - a Filipina girl is one person who easily cries out whether she feels upset, hurt, disappointed, angry, and even happy. Crying is her defense mechanism to release her emotion. Put her in a tearjerker love story, I bet you...she will be weeping, so keep a tissue box ready!
- **Cleanliness and orderliness** - she wants to keep herself and her surrounding spic and span. A Filipina girl is very particular with basic hygiene, proper grooming, and maintaining order in her home and at work. She knows how to prioritize things and

keep things moving according to set guidelines and timetables. After all, Filipinos are born-achievers!
- *Loyalty and devotion - once she falls into a relationship, she will make sure that she will give out her best and even go the extra mile to make it work. expect a one-man-woman out of her as she maintains high moral values and recognizes her self worth. She can be very sacrificial, loving, responsible, and forgiving, but don't mess up with her- otherwise, she will disappear like a bubble, poof!"*

2. WHAT SHOULD A MAN SAY TO APPROACH A FILIPINA?

A Filipina does not want surprises from a stranger. If a man is introduced to her by a common friend/relative or somebody she knows, then it will be easier to approach her. Initially, she will be very shy and aloof, but once you scratch her surface, she is very sweet, loving, and passionate. Some effective tongue-twister Tagalog words a man can say will be:
- *Good morning/evening/night (as the case maybe) = 'magandang umaga/hapon/gabi'*
- *May I introduce myself? = 'pwedeng magpakilala?'*
- *May I know your name = 'anong pangalan mo?'*
  - *I am (give your name) = 'ako si _____'*
  - *You are beautiful = 'ang ganda mo'*

(Ming's Hint: You must make sure she is Filipina before you say the above phrases or you will look like a man with bad judgment: a very bad case of the "Asian fetish" or worse. Do not use these as pick-up lines, but instead to impress her after you've spoken with her for at least a few days.)

3. WHAT DOES A FILIPINA WANT IN A MAN?

She would definitely want to be taken seriously, and desires men who are not into any games as she doesn't intend to play games. Time and effort given to her will make a lot of difference, as she will value them dearly. She looks for a man who can share her joys and pains, her hopes and dreams, and her future. A man who is responsible, capable of giving undivided love and attention, and who understands that sacrifices and compromises makes up for building a blissful relationship.

4. WHERE CAN MEN MEET FILIPINA WOMEN?

Since most Filipinos love to sing, dance, and eat, the best bets to find them are in karaoke bars, or disco pubs. Surely, you'll also find them in Filipino gatherings, like local fiesta/bazaars/restaurants and the like. Another place to meet them is after a mass during Sundays. Since most Filipinos are church-going, they're likely to be active too in church like choir, usherette, or any service.

5. WHAT ARE SOME PUBLICATIONS MEN CAN ADVERTIZE IN AND FIND OUT MORE ABOUT WHERE THESE KARAOKE BARS AND DISCOS ARE?

I know a Filipino journal called 'FILIPINO REPORTER' (www.Filipinoreporter.com) based in Jersey City; another one is 'JERSEY JOURNAL'.

Some Filipino culture tips are:

Customarily, Filipinas are expected to stay home and the men are the providers of the family. The men are the head of the household and dominate over the women. In the United States nowadays, this may or may not be true. If the situation calls for the woman to stay home and look after the household (kids, husband's chores, etc.), then she has to stay home to accomplish this formidable task.

However, if the situation calls her to help the husband augment the family's income, a Filipina in the U.S. may opt to work. If there is nothing for her to do at home (no kids and husband away for work all the time), then she'll opt again to work rather than stay at home. If her husband prefers her to just simply stay home (which is not the likely thing for an American way of life), and it is a mutual decision of both, then she will stay home. She will make her best effort to make the relationship work by having a mutual understanding at the same time make herself productive in or out, which makes a Filipina different from the others.

Basically, a Filipina is a born achiever and a good provider (emotional and financial stand point of view). She also speaks her mind; she doesn't stay timid and just blindly follow whatever her husband says. She knows what's good for her and her family.

You must respect a Filipina's family and not address her parents by their first names. You should treat the elderly with respect. Try hard to remember each member of the family's name! If addressing an elder, use the term "tita" (female) or "tito" (male), then the name. For example: Tita Ming (Auntie Ming) or Tito Tim (Uncle Tim), if these elders are significantly older, use "lola" (female) or "lolo" (male) before the name, ie: Lola Maria (Grandmother Maria) or "Lolo Robert" (Grandfather Robert). This is a good sign of respect and everyone will be delighted. However, don't be too comfortable with calling the girl's (being pursued) mother as "mom" or "dad" as this will be a blatant sign of arrogance. Take it nice and easy.

If you cannot woo the elders, woo the children; this is a sure bet to get close to the household's heart. The visitor will be long gone, but the children will surely utter his name to remind everyone of his presence and his goodness!

To get on a Filipina's good side, be romantic and nice. When visiting a Filipino home, it is advisable to bring along some small token of presents or goodies like a basket of fruits, a tempting cake or a box of candies/chocolates. The stomach is the shortcut to the household's heart. The members of the family will surely remember very well a visitor who's thoughtful and generous.

It is also wise to offer help to ongoing activity, if any, in the household. For instance, during a town fiesta or somebody's birthday, offer to help cut vegetables, light a fire (if wooden logs are used), or butcher a chicken(!); everyone will certainly remember a visitor who's been so cooperative and so ever willing to belong to the family.

Be chivalrous: the closest path to any Filipina girl's heart is to show good manners and right conduct. Be particular in opening the door for her, take her arm when crossing the street, open the car door first for her to get in, etc." L., age 42, NJ.

FILIPINO-AMERICANS

Since most Filipino-Americans speak English when they first arrive in the United States, they are easily assimilated into American society. According to the U.S. Census, the most Filipino-American populated states are:

California; Hawaii, Illinois, New York, New Jersey, Washington, Virginia, Texas, Florida and Maryland.

For a list of websites for Filipino-American groups, events and culture, visit: http://directory.google.com/Top/Society/Ethnicity/Asian/Asian-American/Filipino_American/

VISITING A FILIPINO HOME

Take off your shoes before entering a Filipino home. When greeting elders, hold their right hand and bring it to your forehead while bowing a bit and say *"Mano po."*

When visiting a Filipino home, it is advisable to bring along some small token of presents or goodies like a basket of fruits, a delicious cake or a box of candies/chocolates. The stomach is the shortcut to the household's heart. The members of the family will surely remember very well a visitor who is thoughtful and generous. Filipinos are very food-oriented, and an offer of food is an offer of friendship, so never refuse an offer of food. Remove your hat before sitting down to eat. Never blow your nose or sing at the table. Help clear the dishes and be as helpful as possible.

When leaving a Filipino home, make sure to say goodbye to everyone, especially the elders.

RECOMMENDED READING FOR UNDERSTANDING FILIPINO CULTURE:

Filipinas Magazine
    http://www.Filipinasmag.com.

Filipino American Lives (Asian American History and Culture) by
    Yen Le Espiritu

Passport Philippines: Your Pocket Guide to Filipino Business, Customs & Etiquette (Passport to the World),
    by Luis H. Francia, Barbara Szerlip

THAI CULTURE

Thai culture is influenced by Buddhism and there are Thai temples located in Los Angeles, San Francisco, Denver, Utah, Washington D.C., Chicago, New York, Florida, and Houston. Traditional Thai art, literature and customs are all developed around religion.

THAI-AMERICANS

To learn about Thai-Americans, surf to the following sites:

Association of Thai Professionals in America and Canada
    http://www.atpac.org/

Thai American Young Professionals Organization
http://www.taypa.org/

For a good site on places to visit in Oregon to learn more about Thai culture, surf to http://www.Thaioregon.com, where you can learn the Thai language.

THAI CULTURAL RESOURCES

Here are some books you can read to find out more about Thai culture:

Passport Thailand: Your Pocket Guide to Thai Business, Customs & Etiquette (Passport to the World) by Naomi Wise

Thai for Beginners Book and Tape Set
    Audio Cassette (February 15, 2000) Paperback - 262 pages (April 1, 1995)

Rosetta Stone: Thai Explorer
    Fairfield Language Technologies
CD ROM for learning the Thai language

In the Bedroom Out of Trouble, by Bud Knackstedt
    Contains cultural taboos, personal profile questionnaires and an extensive appendix with words unavailable in other language books.

Thai for Lovers, by Nit and Jack Agee, Paiboon Publishing, Paperback - *Thai for Lovers* includes flirting and love-making phrases. R-rated.

A good Website for discussing anything Thai, including relationships and immigration, is http://forums.delphiforums.com/ThaiFalang/start. The forums are very well-moderated, and anything inappropriate is removed.

PART 3

HOW TO ATTRACT ASIAN WOMEN

CHAPTER 9

How to Enchant and Flatter that Special Asian Woman

Prepare Yourself to be as Attractive as Possible

Hair: Get a good haircut. If you are thin on top, that is perfectly all right. Many women don't mind men with thinning hair; to them, it's a fact of life. However, it is a big no-no for you to try to cover up your baldness with a toupee. First of all, women can always tell if you are wearing a toupee. Second, it gives the impression that you are trying to cover up something you are ashamed of and so makes you look dishonest. So, dump that toupee and show the world you are great and bald! There are lots of sexy bald men; think Captain Pickard, Kojak, Anthony Edwards, Michael Jordan… the list goes on. Also, I have not come across many Asian women who like long hair on a man. So cut your hair at the usual length for the conventional male short haircut.

Skin: Make sure your skin is as good as it can be. If you have acne, go to a dermatologist. One person who has suffered from acne all her life was cured when her dermatologist put her on the miraculous acne fighting combination of Erythromycin and sulfur cream.

Hygiene: Make sure your breath is as nice as it can be. A Taoist sex secret I learned from Valentin Chu's book, *The Yin-Yang Butterfly: Ancient Chinese Sexual Secrets for Western Lovers*, is to roll your tongue around in your mouth to stimulate saliva production. Saliva cleans your mouth of bacteria and bad breath and has the additional health benefit of stimulating your digestion. Mr. Chu reports that there have been sex hormones found in saliva and recommends that you continue stimulating your saliva production until you have drunk many cups of saliva a day. While I don't know about drinking so huge quantities of saliva, I do know that rolling your tongue in your mouth is a good trick to prevent bad breath prior to talking to or kissing your Asian love interest.

Your Dress: You should appear presentable and neat. Therefore, dress accordingly, preferably in suit and tie or in other nice clothing on your first few dates. I think many guys have different definitions of what are "nice" clothes. In my opinion, button-down shirts; nice dress shirts of cashmere, cotton, or merino wool-type material; dress pants, khakis, and non-torn jeans all qualify as "nice" clothes. Stick with designers like CK, DKNY, Armani, Hugo Boss, and stores like Banana Republic for a nice, hip look that many Asians sport themselves. Wear urban clothes with a sleeker look and tighter fit as opposed to baggy clothes.

What Asian Women Really Want in Men

Guys Who are Good Matches for Them

Many Asian women have emailed me and told me that they want to be viewed as real people, and not as stereotypical Asian women. These women feel offended when men target them for their ethnicity. They feel that race is not the most important thing; what's important to them is that two human individuals are compatible with each other.

Educated Guys

Education is extremely valued in Asian cultures. Many Asian parents drill the importance of education into their children's minds from the time of their early childhood until the time they enter college. Therefore, your chances of attracting an Asian female would be better if you have a college degree or better. There are things you can say and do to appear more educated, including:

- Mention the schools you attended and degrees you have obtained. Women I interviewed say they are particularly impressed by men who mention they have MBAs, JDs, and Ivy League educations. Also, if you take a look at the *World Journal*, ads by matchmaking agencies often mention that they have male clients who are doctors, lawyers, and other respected professionals in order to attract more Asian women. Be shameless in namedropping and in bragging about your hard-earned education and qualifications. Toot your own horn!
- Dress professionally. Do not dress sloppily; a suit and tie on a first date (if you meet after work especially) is a good idea.
- Behave with good manners. Speak politely and treat your dates with respect. This includes not using any Asian language pick-up lines and not using the word "Oriental" in describing Asians.

California and New York universities have many Asian students and are great places to meet Asian women. You are in the same classes and meet everyday, so start a conversation with the Asian students in your class. Student lounges and libraries are excellent places to meet people too. Some of the best universities, particularly those in California and New York, admit a large number of Asian students (up to 25% of the student population in some universities). The percentage of Asian students is even higher in foreign students' programs.

Polite Guys

You should approach and treat women with respect and dignity. Do not speak rudely or embarrass them in any way. Always be gentle in your manners and words.

Respectful Guys

Many Asian women I spoke to complained that men approach them in disrespectful ways, often using pick-up lines that are degrading to their sense of gender and ethnicity. Some men treat the instant message chat vehicles of the Internet as a way to get some instantaneous satisfaction for their libidos. Asian women do not appreciate such rude pick-up lines. Therefore, you should treat women with the utmost respect and dignity if you want to attract Asian women. Always be a perfect gentleman, even under the protective anonymity of the Internet.

Giving Guys

To impress any woman, especially an Asian woman, it is always important to be generous with your praise, time, and love. This will encourage the woman to reciprocate and treat you nicely as well. It is very important that you do not insist that you split the check down the middle every time you go out to dinner. This is simply unromantic and even disrespectful toward women. A lot of Asian women have traditional values when it comes to dating and relationships and therefore expect the man to perform his traditional duties. Paying for most of their date expenses is one of them. For example, take a look at Http://www.Cupidsworld.com, a Website by Asian matchmaker, Mei Yang. In the "Dating Etiquette" section of her Website, Ms. Yang lists the frequently asked questions and concerns of her Asian female clients. One of them includes a complaint about a guy who asked the lady to split the check, seemingly on the first date, which made her never want to see him again. Ms. Yang's response to this lady was that in American society it is common for people to go Dutch. Now, if this Asian matchmaker needs to explain to some Asian ladies that women are expected to pay for half of the bill on dates, it probably means that in Asian cultures the lady is not supposed to pay. Do not let money stand in the way of romance. If you can afford it, try to treat the lady to nice dates whenever possible. If you cannot afford it, let her know ahead of time, and do things that cost less money.

Romantic Guys

Many Asian women told me that they love a man who is romantic. What makes a man romantic? Here are some suggestions:

1. Find out all about your lady's likes and dislikes, and try to give her what she wants. Being romantic is being considerate toward her and caring about how she feels. Being romantic means treating her like a queen. If she likes flowers, then bring her flowers often. If she likes jazz, then play jazz whenever you can. You get the idea.

2. Take her out to a romantic restaurant. Research the restaurant beforehand to make sure it is dimly lit, has a nice ambiance, nice music and the type of food that she likes.

3. If you are dating on a regular basis, call her up often, just because. How often? Use your judgment. You should be able to sense if your calls are welcomed just from her tone of voice. Many women love the attention and complain that men do not call them enough. Don't be afraid of paying her too much attention. You can tell if your attention is unwanted. If she is responsive to you, then keep on calling!

4. Familiarize yourself with Asian culture and food to show her that you care about her background. Also, try to learn a few words and phrases in whatever Asian language your lady speaks to score extra points with her. However, do not use Asian language pick-up lines.

Humorous Guys

Women love guys who can make them laugh. Some guys are naturally funny, and they get the best women. If you feel you are not good at telling jokes, try to lighten up a bit and be in a good mood most of the time. This will help you attract women and get through hard times during your relationship.

Clean Guys

Many Asian women I interviewed emphasized the fact that they are attracted to clean-smelling and clean-looking men. In fact, one lady mentioned that she was really turned off by greasy men. I think many Asian females tend to like guys who are not super-hairy, are well-shaved, clean-cut, shower every day, and who have clear skin.

Your Occupation

The occupations that Asian females I interviewed listed as what they preferred in their ideal men include:

Doctor
Lawyer
Engineer
Architect
Business Owner
Computer Expert
Military Officer
Independently Wealthy

It should be noted, however, that ambition and drive are more important than the specific occupation that you are in. Therefore, being a driven, ambitious car mechanic beats being an unemployed, disgruntled lawyer when it comes to attracting Asian women.

ASIAN WOMEN SPEAK OUT ABOUT THEIR IDEAL MEN

"White, Caucasian, warm and flexible personality, lean, sporty with sex appeal, financially stable, who works in the finance, business, economic or medical field like doctors or engineers or architects." Renee, age 32, NY.

"Caucasian, salary of $50,000 or more, professional, witty and honest, attractive...bachelor's degree or higher, need someone with brain, interests and substance." Betty, age 23, CA.

"My ideal man is Caucasian, probably English or American. I'm not looking for a grossly rich man, but he has to be able to make it on his own and support himself. His occupation is whatever makes him happy, because being in an unhappy job makes for an unfulfilling life. With regards to personality, I want what every woman wants: a glowing, smiling, positive person, who is able to bounce back from hard times. Someone who is fun and talkative, yet gentle at times, is ideal. Physically, I like an attractive man with bright eyes and a good sense of humor, which makes him even more gorgeous." Kate, age 25, MA.

"Must be Tall, Dark and Handsome... At least 50% Italian, bodybuilder physique, great sense of humor, sensitive, intelligent, good conversationalist, family-oriented, caring, loving, goofy, fun....Prefer white-collar men......" Karen, age 26, NY.

"I've always been attracted to dark/black hair, olive/dark skin, and big brown eyes (especially long-haired Latin and Asian men with muscular/athletic bodies). Being an artist, I'm more concerned about passion rather than wealth. As long as the men can support themselves, save money, afford to take me out every once in a while, and not be afraid of hard work (and family), I'll love him middle class any day. Also, because I'm an artist, I'm quite fond of other artists, especially musicians (because it's not my field of art, yet I so adore music)." Monique, age 34, CA.

"My ideal man is not limited to one race... he can be any type of race. His income? He has to make money. He doesn't have to make a whole lot of money, just enough to support himself because I'm not going to. I support myself. He has to be successful or at least good at his job. If not good at his job he has to have some sort of drive. He can't be lazy in the least bit. As far as personality goes, my ideal would be someone who's honest with a sense of humor (hopefully goofy), someone who's not fake or needs to impress other people. Physical characteristics... Well, I need to be able to look at them and like their face and as far as body goes... my ideal would be kind of big but lean... big-boned pretty much but not obese... don't really like skinny little dudes." T.Y., age 40, TX.

"My ideal man is a polite, educated, and decent-looking person. I prefer clean-cut hair, clean-looking in general, and someone who knows how to dress. His height should range from 5'8" to about 5'10". Personality wise, he should be considerate and humorous, can make up his own mind, and generous. He should be focused in life and know what he has to do to achieve his goals." I.R., age 34, NJ.

"An ideal man for me would be a Japanese guy 5'7" or taller, someone that's out of school with at least a decent job, nice personality, sense of humor, medium skin (tanned), big eyes, etc." R.T., age 25, MA.

"My ideal man, though I don't believe he exists for me, is white, about 5'9" - 5'10", has blonde or light-

brown hair, blue or green eyes, a great smile, and takes good care of his body and manages his appearance well (he must have a nice tight body — no fatties allowed), he has to have a great sense of humor (I love to laugh!), career-driven is a must (hopefully makes at least $80,000/year), smart, he has to love kids, be compassionate and romantic, loves to dine out, loves the arts (musicals, ballet, etc), likes music and likes to dance." S.R., age 32, CT.

"My ideal man would be Caucasian or any other race but Asian. His income would have to be at or above mine. Occupation doesn't really matter as long as the income is at or above mine and he enjoys the career he has chosen. His personality traits would have to include sensitivity, honesty, loyalty, romance, humor, ability to communicate and compromise, understanding, and sympathy. His physical traits are not that important; of course I have to be attracted to him somewhat, but he doesn't have to have a 6-pack as long as he does what's necessary to be in shape." B.T., age 26, NY.

"Physical characteristics...I like my men tall..at least 5'10" - 6'2". I love guys with dark hair and blue eyes, nice lean build, not skinny, not fat..just right." M.M., age 29, MI.

"Now what kind of personality attracts me? Well, to be honest, I'm not into that "kind, gentle, loving crap." That's, um, somewhat unrealistic. I'm attracted to guys with brains. Looks aren't too important, but minimum decent, cause I DO have to look at him. Now when I say smart, it isn't necessarily "school smart." He can be really good at something, like computers, or fixing cars, anything and I'd consider him smart. Some sort of talent you know." L.E., age 22, NY.

"Handsome, cute, smart, funny, romantic, gentle, loving, understanding, loyal, athletic, have beautiful eyes, beautiful teeth, college-graduated, and have high income." Lily, age 35, NY.

"My ideal man is white, who earns enough not to worry about it, his career can be anything as long as he enjoys it, and is fun, confident, sexy, passionate, compassionate and athletic." K.L., age 29, CA.

"My ideal man is smart, educated, and has a lot of a sense of humor. Not a serious type." C.P., age 41, MD.

"My ideal man is someone who is smart, HAS A JOB! (a steady income that is not due to illegal activity, i.e. drug dealing, stealing, etc.) knows exactly what he wants out of life... and has to be at least partly handsome. I like a man who is honest, who won't CHEAT, and is good in bed. I usually opt for guys with big muscles. Personality is very important though... I want a guy who is caring, sweet, open-minded and into trying new things. He has to be ROMANTIC... I go crazy over that stuff, for example: roses... love notes... gifts for no reason. Most importantly, he has to have a sense of humor. I like guys that are laid back and not uptight... I want someone that I can just hang out with and not feel weird. SO I guess he has to be a friend before he can be a lover. He has to have at least a high school diploma (I mean C'mon)... but I do prefer a man with a degree or higher." N.N., age 25, NY.

"My ideal man is Asian. (I don't know why, but I prefer to date a man in my own race.) He should be 5'7-6'0, he doesn't have to be built, but I don't want him to be fat or anything; he has to be easy-going and someone I can talk to, and well- educated with a good steady job." Nell, age 28, NY.

"Black, Latino, or white, should be an executive, good-looking, tall, successful." Ann, age 27, HI.

"Mostly I'm attracted to Caucasian men; income and occupation doesn't really matter as long as they have a job that makes more than enough money to pay living expenses; personality—definitely sincerity, thoughtfulness, a sense of humor, adventurous, good manners; physical characteristics would be someone good-looking or attractive, no beer belly, physically fit, dark hair, clean-cut." Gail, age 30, IL.

"Caucasian, black, income not all that matters but must be a hard-working man, humorous, good steady job, tall, nice-classy dressing (J.Crew, Banana R., Kenneth, etc), good overall person." Grace, age 23, NY.

"Asian or White, $50,000+ per year, professional, business owner, or independently wealthy, nice, kind, generous, educated, eclectic tastes, sharp dresser, likes to go shopping, fine dining, does not smoke, minimal if at all drinker, agreeable, intelligent, sophisticated, well-traveled and healthy, not necessarily extreme sports but has same interests as I do, cooking, eating, movies, theatre, singing, dancing, swimming, boogie-boarding, walking in beautiful places, clean living." R.N., age 20, HI.

"WHITE.........WHITE...WHITE!!!....I actually don't date black or Asian men. I never have, don't think I will. I have never been physically attracted to them and, well, personality-wise, I just never seem to click with them. I date some Latinos as well, but I frequently prefer Englishmen; I like English, Irish and Scottish accents. The income should be 50's and above, though occupation is not important as long as he is in this white-collar job. I like an honest, caring, thoughtful, outgoing person." Gina, age 23, VA.

"I prefer Latino men, and I don't care if he makes very little money—which is unusual compared to my other Asian girl friends who always talk about how much men have to make. It really turns me off that women rely on men's income. As long as men have a job that helps society or people or anything to do with a good cause, I respect the profession. I dated a bond trader who only made his living by the movement of the market, no humanity was involved and I didn't like that at all. Of course, the man has to be kind and gentle, and I like someone younger and a bit submissive—but that is me. I hate "Old"-looking men. They like Asian women because we look younger but they don't put the same standard on themselves. I like men with less body hair and an athletic body. The hair on their back makes me cringe." Mayling, age 32, NY.

"My ideal man is someone who is taller than me, white, black, Asian, Italian, Greek, someone who gets paid enough to keep him going, medium build, not too skinny and not too buff or fat, occupation doesn't matter unless they are working in a fast-food joint (then "no"), nice teeth, good hair, knows how to dress, funny, smart, patient, knows what he wants." R.T., age 33, DE.

"My ideal man is just someone I can get along with as a great friend and has things in common with me. There's no real specific race, since we're all human. ...at least, I hope. Hopefully they have intelligence and some common sense (Why do they have one and not the other most of the time?) I don't worry about looks, because superficiality is for the weak. On the other hand, I don't think I'd date someone who was a peg leg, had one eye, and was missing three fingers! But the ideal, mundane, generic human." P.W., age 30, NY.

"I DON'T HAVE AN "IDEAL" MAN. I HAVE DATED ALL RACES AND TYPES. RACE NOR INCOME NOR OCCUPATION MATTERS TO ME. HIS PERSONALITY IS ONE THAT HAS TO CLICK WITH MINE AND HAS GOOD PHYSICAL CHARACTERISTICS. WELL IT'S SUPERFICIAL BUT I LIKE THEM FIT, MOSTLY SO THEY CAN GET ME INTO SHAPE." Tina, age 27, NY.

"Race-American, Asian or Hispanic; income-they should be able to support family and be responsible, sweet loving, caring personality, but still strong and authoritative but not demanding, mind of his own and be able to communicate. Creative and not self centered but does care enough about himself to take care of himself, has manners but also knows how to relax and enjoy life." Jackie, age 31, CA.

"Caucasian, warm and flexible personality, lean, sporty with sex appeal, financially stable, finance, business, economic field or medical field like doctors or engineers or architects. Race: white. Income: at least $75,000/yr. Occupation: of course, they'd have to be professional. Personality: down-to-earth, open-minded, kind, thoughtful, considerate, expressive, and mostly, a gentleman. Physical characteristics: handsome, tall (at least 6'), slim to fit (not skinny), not bald; I don't really care for "Mr. Muscles", just as long as he doesn't have a belly sticking out." C.W., age 32, NY.

"Caucasian, Taiwanese or Hong Kong American (a Chinese-American from the above regions), over $100,000, professional job (like lawyer, doctor, MBA manager, Computer engineer), 5'10-6', 170-180 lbs." D.D., age 29, NY.

"Intelligent, witty, open-minded, goal-oriented, independent, creative, has a slight "bad boy" streak;

tall, tan, dark-haired, attractive, nicely dressed, someone you can bring in to meet the family." Q.C., age 25, CA.

"My ideal man is Caucasian, with a financially stable job, warm personality, sensitive & tactful, friendly, able to put you at ease when you first meet...physically is tall (minimum 6 inches taller than myself) & medium built/bit muscular, nice large hands, a bit masculine doesn't hurt, & very generous in paying for meals, buys flowers & gifts for the woman sometimes for no reason at all, is on time on dates." R.T., age 30, FL.

"My ideal man would be Caucasian. I have a high preference for Caucasian men...even men with different backgrounds are interesting...Irish, Scottish...etc...As far as his income goes, I would prefer a man that can support himself as well as someone in his life if he was to have one. I don't mean for me to be able to be dependent on him, just not to the point where I have to support him. Stability is a turn-on. His occupation does not matter...personality does though. Any man that can make me laugh...not at my own expense...harhar...is best. I think a man must be my best friend as well as my lover for us to go any further than just acquaintances. His physique matters as well. I would say it doesn't, but you cannot fool yourself into thinking you can have sex or make love with an unattractive guy...it just goes with the rest of him. I'm not looking for a model...all I ask is that he is taller than me...preferably 5 or 6 inches....and that...every time I look at him, I fall in love with him all over again." Anna, age 29, OH.

"My ideal man will be either Asian or Caucasian. What he makes or does really makes no difference as long as it is legal and he can provide a comfortable

living for me and our family. I like a man who is sincere, generous, funny, outgoing, honest, and open-minded. I want someone whose height is between 5'8" to 6'0", with a medium build." Nancy, age 30, TX.

"My ideal man is college-educated, professional with an income of about $80,000 to $250,000 a year. White, hair color does not matter, but I like light- eyed men. (i.e. blue, gray, hazel, green...) I like them stocky between 5' 10" to 6'. Preferably not cheap! Who has good communication skills, at least has bachelor degree, sensitive to woman's mind and knows how to respect it, and has nice sense of humor." L.G., age 30, IL.

"My ideal man is Caucasian, intelligent, very successful and ambitious, preferably with a six-figure income. Exact occupation does not matter so much as it is one that requires intelligence and some mental challenge. He is grounded in good morals and values, and his conscience dictates right from wrong. He is well-rounded, has a great outgoing and gregarious personality, quick wit, and great sense of humor. He is tall, preferably 5'11" or taller, handsome, and very physically fit. Specific characteristics, such as eye or hair color, are not relevant as long as the overall package is easy on the eyes." L.D., age 31, CA.

"About the body, definitely don't want a guy who is skinnier than me! Makes me feel like crap. He can't be too skinny, and being fat is a "no-no." Chubby, well, is almost out there with being fat, but it all depends on the guy himself, such as his looks, personality, etc. Out of my 20 something boyfriends, only one of them was somewhat chubby, but he was kind of cute, real sweet, nice, and his face wasn't fat- looking. I think that's how he passed the test. His face is what I have to deal with looking at most of the time, and it passed the test. Also the man has got to know how to dress, he

don't need to be GQ model, but at least "GAP" you know." Lisa, age 30, NC.

"My ideal man is a white boy...dirty blond hair..blue eyes..about..6'-6'2...um..medium built...built like a swimmer...nice and toned ..not pale..but not real tan...like a natural everyday tan...income....not a big issue...I'm very well-off..so I don't need a guy who is gonna try to buy the whole world for me..that's NOT what I'm looking for...but he's gotta have a nice steady job...a job that could take care of his family...or in school...personality...boy next-door with a twist of the wild side...like I need a partner in crime...not a study buddy..someone who will go out with me and do spontaneous things...I don't need another "father type." ...Physical characteristics....two words...NICE HAIR....I like those spiky hair boys...hair is always the FIRST thing I notice about a guy...no nice hair...then bub-bye! ....like I said...I like them toned..like built like a swimmer...lifeguard style...that's damn hot....and..hehe...there's this crease on a man's body that just drives me insane...I'm not sure what its called....but I call it the "sexy man line" hahaha...its the crease on each side of them that goes down to their groin area...damn...that's hot...but not TOO creased..like D'Angelo...blah! hehehe..and I like nice broad shoulders and cut arms..not muscular..but cut...yumyum..but all that is too good to be true!" Pam, age 24, NY.

"My ideal guy would be over 5'11, white, not religious, no excess baggage attached (i.e. kids, crazy ex's, etc.), professional career, makes me laugh 24/7, skinny or athletic, and I prefer blondes...." Jen, age 29, AZ.

"I prefer white, Hispanic, or multi-racial men, but if someone looks good or is irresistible, race doesn't matter. Humorous, easy-going, attractive, intelligent. Someone who has goals in their life." G.G., age 28, CA.

"He is passionate, intelligent, attractive, compassionate and capable of challenging my mind." Deb, age 34, GA.

"Race: Caucasian, African-American, multi-racial. Income: $60,000 + Occupation: No preference, as long as he can hold a job." J.C., age 25, CA.

"My ideal man would be my age or younger, Caucasian, no preference on income and occupation (I can hold my own), funny, open-minded and laidback personality and VERY good-looking. The first thing that turns me off is older guys, about 10-20 years older than me, automatic delete." Mary, age 22, NY.

"Race does not matter. An ideal man would have a job and an income and would not be a bum. Physical characteristics that appeal to me are a man that is taller than me, has eyes with windows to his soul and has hair on his head that I can run my fingers through. An ideal personality would be a caring, considerate individual with a sense of humor." Laura, age 28, MN.

"White male taller than me with blue eyes and blond hair like a Ken doll. I would like him to have a good income that can support a family just in case I would like to marry him. I would like him to have a white-collar occupation like doctor, lawyer, something in computers or business, or maybe military officer." Elle, age 25, NY.

"Caucasian (white), income & occupation doesn't matter, sweet, honest, respectful, down-to-earth, artistic, music-lover, sports-lover, open-minded, NOT

SUPERFICIAL, appreciative, slender or athletic, that's about it. White/fair complexion with darker features (hair, eyes etc.) Well, my ideal man would have to be financially stable, have a job that doesn't require a lot of traveling, not obese or too thin, and has to have a great personality. I especially like a man who has a great sense of humor, who is a romantic, sincere, faithful, honest, affectionate, loving, and passionate. Race is really not a factor to me, but if I had to pick one or two that really stand out, it would be Caucasian or Asian." Luna, age 31, NY.

CHAPTER 10

How to Meet Asian Women on the Internet

There are lots of Asian women on the Internet, so you can meet many Asian women from the comfort of your own home.

AsianSocials.com is an Asian & American Professionals Network that will soon feature a searchable database and special chatting features.

What to Write When Responding to an Asian Woman's Personals Ad

1. Don't Mention that She is Asian

Be original and don't say in the email that you are attracted to Asian women. Almost all of my Asian female interviewees complained that one of the first things men say to them either in person or on the Internet is that they like Asian women.

Please, guys—by saying that, you make her feel that being Asian is the ONLY thing going for her! Instead, I suggest you keep your first few conversations with an Asian woman race-neutral. Believe me, you will stand out in her mind because you will be one of the few men who did not mention that she is Asian.

2. Always Include Your Picture When Responding to an Ad

Let's face it: You have a lot of competition when it comes to Internet dating. This is particularly true if you are a guy. Since women receive more responses than they can handle when they put up a personals ad on the Internet, you have to give them a reason to write back to you. The best way to do this is to include a picture in your response. You should hire a professional photographer to take some good headshots so that you will be putting your best face forward. Do not send a photograph of you in a T-shirt or casual clothing, especially to the more mature Asian ladies. Some Asian ladies put a lot of emphasis on a man's appearance, and you want to appear to be a professional man of substance and character. Therefore, dress in a suit and tie when getting your photo taken for better responses to your emails.

Note: When using AOL, use the Insert Picture button (with the camera icon) so the recipient does not have to go through the extra step of downloading your picture. Or email from Yahoo and your picture will be shown automatically and people can scan your photo for viruses with Norton. Better yet, build your own website! This way, you can include most of your personal information and your photos on the site and save a lot of time and effort. Also, the person who receives your reply does not have to worry about downloading a virus. There are lots of sites that offer free websites: AOL, Geocities, Homestead, Tripod, etc. You can build a site in minutes.

Read the lady's ad and respond only if you meet her requirements. This cannot be emphasized enough. If she is saying that she wants a man of a certain age, height, income, race, whatever, you need to listen to her. These are her requirements and you are only wasting your time if you write to her as a person who does not meet her specifications.

If you email someone whose criteria you do not meet, sometimes she may be nice and email you back and get your hopes up. But in her mind you are not the one, and you will probably never get to meet her.

"Since my ad has been posted I've had a lot of responses, a lot that do not come close to what I put as my match. For instance, I put a certain age range, 21-27, and I get responses from men that disregard that— I've had 50-year- olds emailing me, and when I turn them down they tell me: but I'm fit. I don't care if you're fit or not, you're like my dad. I wish men would listen to what I wrote or keep it in mind so they don't wonder why they don't get a response from me. I also put that I don't want any Asians and I've been getting a lot of those, so as soon as I see them say Asian, I delete it, I don't even bother with it. Please let them know to pay attention to the match characteristics." Anna, age 21, CA.

"First of all, he should know about his situation. I dislike any men with kids or who've been divorced since I've never been married and have no kids. Also dislike men who are too old, like 40-80. (I even got a 100-year-old grandfather's love e-mail at my posted ad on single's website. Most men who responded had a bad condition. I dislike bald, pervert, short or too tall, too old or young, uneducated, not decent job, stingy, etc.) If a good-conditioned guy approached me, I would be happy to be approached." Fay, age 29, NY.

3. Write a Friendly, Short Note that Includes Something About You

It's very important to include some vital statistics such as your:

Age
Height
Eye and Hair Color
Profession

Location
Interests
Type of Relationship You Are Seeking

List your statistics vertically so that it is simple to read.

Amy, 29, a single Asian female in New York says: *"I hate it when a guy just writes 'I would like to get to know you...' without sending a picture or anything else. I know you would like to get to know me, but give me reasons to want to know you! I've received quite a few responses like this and every time I get it, I just delete it."*

4. Don't Write a Book

A person who has 20 emails to read does not want to read your beautiful 7-paragraph essay about your philosophy of life. Keep it to one or two paragraphs.

5. One Email Address Per Email!

Can you believe that there are some people who will respond to ten personal ads with one email—with all ten email addresses visible to the recipients? This happens a lot, and it does not look good for the person responding to the ad. We know it's a numbers game and that you don't have a lot of time, but emailing AsianSexxy35, Orchidflower, and Fitnfly all at once in one email will get you no responses from all three. A lady wants to feel like she's special. Yahoo allows you to send blind carbon copies of email to people, so try using Yahoo if you have a lot of emails to send.

6. Sound Nice

It's very important to be courteous and not criticize the woman. There are some guys who think sounding macho and intimidating to an Asian woman will attract her to him. Unless the woman has extremely low self-esteem, being nasty to an Asian female will not make her go out with you. Also, write in complete sentences and watch your spelling.

7. Do Not Talk About Sex or Her Body

Most women get turned off if you start talking about sex in your first emails to her. Remember the following rule: if you don't want someone to say something to your mother, daughter, or sister, then don't say it to someone else's mother, daughter or sister. Your first emails should be friendly with no mention of sex, her body, or her ethnicity. Above all else, do not make it obvious that you are only after sex, unless her ad specifically says that she is only interested in a casual sexual relationship. Refer to the "Things You Should Never Say to an Asian Lady" chapter in this book for more things not to say to an Asian lady.

8. Do Not Bombard an Asian Lady with Instant Messages.

Remember, if you are aggressive with the IMs, you run the risk of getting blocked (this is when a woman blocks your email address so that you cannot instant message her anymore), or even worse, alienating her. It's better to just send an unobtrusive email with your photo and then wait and see what happens.

> Tania, 25, in New Jersey: *"It's really annoying and desperate when someone IMs you all the time, even after you've ignored him on several occasions. I'm very busy and when I go online, I'm usually doing some work. If I wanted to chat, I would go to a chatroom. One guy I kept on ignoring actually had the nerve to write:"Why are you being so rude?" That angered me. He was infringing on my time and privacy. Sometimes I got several IMs all at once. I wound up blocking everyone except those people on my buddy list."*

9. Respond to Lots of Ads

You can't tell everything about a person from just one picture and profile. Perhaps she is seeing other people, or is too busy to spend too much time talking to you. The trick is to meet as many people as possible. This way, you will always have someone to email, chat and hang out with.

10. Do Not Put Too Much Emphasis on Photos in Ads

Some Asian women have told me that they are shy and cautious when trying to meet men and that they are less likely to put their photos in ads. Therefore, you should respond to ads without photos as well as those with photos. You might be surprised at how great the lady looks in person if you get the chance to meet her!

11. If At First You Don't Succeed, Email, Email Again!

People like people who are truly interested in them. So if there is someone you would really like to get to know, then send that person another email if you don't get a response right away. However, if she still does not respond to your second email, then you might not want to be too pushy. Move on to someone who IS interested in you!

Creating Your Own Personals Ad

Men get fewer responses to their personals ads than women, but you should put up an ad anyway because you will get responses. Here are some tips on creating your own personals ad:

1. Create several versions of your ad. Advertisers often run different ads to see which one pulls the best, so you might want to consider different ads and see which ones work best for you.
2. Write the way you talk and let your sense of humor show through.
3. Do not be negative. Write what you are seeking in a woman instead of what you are not seeking. Write "I am looking for a woman who is beautiful both on the inside and outside" instead of "No uglies please."

4. You must include a photo in your ad. There are lots of ads posted by other men and the ones that get the most responses all have photos. Your photo should be in the ".jpg" format for best results.
5. Include your vital statistics and detailed information about your interests, job, life, likes and dislikes. The more you write, the better your responses.
6. Watch your spelling. Many women get turned off if there are too many spelling errors.

How to Respond to Telephone Personals

Telephone personals are more competitive because you need to persuade a woman to call you back by phone (more time and effort necessary than that required in replying to an email). To get more call backs from your telephone personals responses, keep the following in mind:

1. Make a list of what makes you desirable (such as the fact that you are gainfully employed, handsome, fun, interesting, tall, unique) before you call. Speak in a clear voice and give reasons for her to call you back. Be really charming so that she'll want to call you anyway, regardless of what you exactly have to say.
2. Sound upbeat, happy and, most of all, friendly!
3. Read the ad and respond accordingly. If she says she is athletic and enjoys opera, and you do too, then say so in the recording.
4. If the lady says she wants a man of a certain ethnicity in her ad, which is often the case, do not leave a message just to tell her how she should be more open to dating other races. These phone calls are expensive at $1.99+ a minute; you will only be wasting your time and money if she wants a man of a certain type and you do not fit the bill. If you just want to vent, that's up to you, but why not concentrate on more positive things and focus on people who will appreciate you just the way you are?
5. Again, mind your manners and keep it polite, clean, and race-neutral.

CHAPTER 11

How To Approach An Asian Lady

Be Brave! Be Brave! Be Brave!

I cannot stress this enough: you won't get the woman if you don't approach her. Some Asian women are shy and will never come up to you. So nothing will happen if you don't try. Also, I asked many Asian women what was the number one thing that would discourage them from forming relations with men; the overwhelming majority of the Asian women answered, "They probably would not find me attractive." This means that if you do not try to approach the Asian lady of your dreams, she might think that you do not find her attractive, and nothing will happen at all.

Let me give you an example: A gentleman who attended one of my AsianSocials.com dating events emailed me and said that he was interested in one of the women he met at the event. Even though this lady had given him her email address and phone number, he "did not want to put her in an uncomfortable position." Knowing that this woman is shy (she is a friend of mine), I told him that if she was interested enough to give him her email address and phone number, then he should call her right away. If he had waited for her to call, nothing would have happened because she was the type of person to wait for the guy to call. Luckily for them both, he took my advice and called her. They are still dating today.

A lot of my male readers tell me that summoning up the courage to talk to a beautiful woman is the hardest thing to do. I understand that approaching women can be daunting, so here are some tips for having more confidence in yourself:

1. Staying physically fit will keep your energy levels high and you will look better as a result. Almost all women love big, strong men with muscles, and you will most definitely feel better about yourself.

2. Listen to positive thinking tapes and use positive imagery (imagine yourself as being confident in approaching women). This may sound really New Agey, but I have had good results with this piece of advice. I told an extremely shy male reader to listen to positive thinking tapes for a month before approaching this woman he had a huge crush on, and he felt so great about himself that he had no trouble going up to her and asking her out. Positive thinking tapes usually tell you to imagine yourself in a situation and see it as you would like it to be. So if you want to approach an Asian woman, then picture yourself smiling, talking to her and asking her out with success. When you are actually asking her out, you will feel more confident, because in your mind's eye you've done it before. The tapes worked miracles for many people, and can work for you, too.

3. List your accomplishments and assets on a piece of paper. Write down everything you are good at, and think of them the next time you want to approach an Asian lady. Remember, you are a great person and she would be lucky to have you!

Most beautiful Asian women complain that men do not approach them as much as these women would like. I suspect that this happens because these women intimidate men. Here's the secret, guys: Go up to an Asian woman and flirt with her; you have nothing to lose! Just the other day, my friend (an attractive Asian model) and I went out to a club, and although we wanted men to come up to us, very few guys did. Sure, they were hovering, looking like they wanted to speak to us, but most couldn't summon up the courage to speak to us. The secret to getting a date with a beautiful Asian woman is to ASK HER OUT! While I was in school, there was this guy who I will call Ed who was not particularly great-looking. He was a struggling student like the rest of us, but he seemed to get the best-looking women to go out with him. I started watching how he approached women, and what I learned from him is what you should do:

1. Smile

Ed's smile was as big as Mr. Ed's and showed as many teeth. When you smile, you release hormones that relax you and make you more confident. Also, people warm up to you immediately when you smile.

2. Make eye contact

Ed would look at women again and again until he caught their attention. He was really obvious about it so it was hard for women to miss.

3. Introduce yourself in a normal way, such as "Hi, how are you? My name is _____."

Ed never had to come up with any corny lines. The friendly, simple approach worked for him just fine. If you think too hard about things to say to impress her, you may think too much and miss the chance to talk to her in the first place. Keep it simple. A "hello" would often do. Many Asian women have emailed me and said they just want to be treated like normal people.

4. Make a woman feel like she's the most beautiful woman in the world, with your smile, mannerisms, and actions

Hold the door for her, offer to buy her a drink, hang her coat up—whatever it takes to make her feel more comfortable. Ed would always do everything possible to make the woman feel special.

5. Treat Her Well

This was Ed's motto. Even though Ed lived in Manhattan, he didn't have a car, and some of his dates lived in Queens or Brooklyn, he would always go pick them up with flowers. This made them feel special.

Continuous, steady attention throughout the "courtship" is required; don't be shy and think she doesn't want you to call. Try calling her often until she gives you the signs that indicate she doesn't want you to call anymore. Ed would call up his love interests at least once a day, if not more often. I swear to you, Ed always had the best-looking women. You might want to call less than once a day to seem more mysterious and intriguing, but do call often.

Be Friendly

Your approach should always be friendly and as nice as possible. Most Asian women, especially if they were born and/or raised in the United States, do not want to be viewed as "Asian" only. We want to be "American," just like everyone else. Therefore, do not use as pickup lines such as "Are you Japanese or Chinese?" or "What is the difference between Chinese women and Korean women?" Some guys think they are being friendly and reaching out to their Asian friends when they say such things, but they are perceived instead as being ignorant and condescending. This one guy, a total stranger in my neighborhood, actually asked me the same questions on two separate occasions, and believe me, I just ignored him while thinking what an idiot he was. Depending on the woman, she may even think you are trying to make her feel bad for being Asian, when your intention is the very opposite. Instead, I suggest a race-neutral approach. Talk about the weather, a book she is holding, and ask her what time it is.

Even if you are intimidated, do not act all macho and start saying obnoxious things to her. Some men have the notion that Asian women are subservient and like to be bossed around. I'm not making this up; here are some opening lines directed toward me from actual men (of course they did not work):

"Do you speak English?"
"Are you Chinese?"
"What is the difference between Korean and Japanese women?"

You MUST NOT, at ANY TIME, use foreign-language pick-up lines in the United States. I cannot stress this enough. You will look like a jerk if you use Chinese on a Korean woman. According to "Parsing Asian America," by Maxie Gondo, (available at http://goldsea.com/AAD/Parsing/parsing.html), 70% of Asians under age 50 who immigrated to the United States 12 or more years ago speak English; approximately 52% of Asian-Americans cannot even converse in an Asian language. This is especially true for younger Asian-Americans, who have the ability to pick up English faster than their parents and other older Asians. This is another illustration of that proverb about sinking or swimming; if you cannot speak English in an English-speaking country such as the United States, how can you even function and survive? Your best bet is to assume that every Asian woman you meet speaks English.

BE RACE-NEUTRAL

Do not say a few words of Japanese or Chinese to an Asian woman as a way to break the ice. First of all, you don't know whether she is Korean or Japanese, and she may get insulted because you assumed she is the nationality you wrongly guessed. Second, sometimes your wrong guess may have the added insult of mistaking an Asian for another kind of Asian she or her group of Asians may harbor historical animosity toward. (Such as Koreans and Japanese.) This makes some women mad because they think that you are trying to make fun of them or that you assume that all Asians look alike.

BEWARE OF PICK-UP LINES

Picture this: you are at a club, and you see this beautiful Asian girl, alone and with a drink in her hand. She puts the wine glass to her lips, and you can't look away. She looks you in the eye, waiting for you to go up and talk to her. Gulp. What do you do? How do you approach her? What do you say?

Do you give her the line about how you love Asian women? She ought to be impressed by that, right? After all, you can't help but notice that she's Asian.

Or maybe you should say something about how sexy Asian women are.

Or perhaps you should tell her you will show her America, since she's Asian and therefore might not have stayed here long enough to know where all the nice places are.

If you have answered "yes" to any of the above, you need to read, reread and memorize this book. If you say any of the above things to an Asian woman, there's a chance that she won't warm up to you, and that your chances with her will be over before she finds out what a great guy you really are. Don't let this happen.

Be Respectful

The number one thing you must remember is to behave like a gentleman. Respect an Asian woman and she will pay more attention to you. You should approach an Asian woman with honesty, respect and dignity.

I read on one of those how-to-get-women-into-bed websites that the best way to get a woman you've just met into bed is to get close and feel her breasts. Get real! That was obviously written by a man for men who want to fantasize that women would enjoy it if they acted rude and felt their breasts a few seconds after meeting them. If a man came up to me and did that, all he'd get is a slap in the face. Remember, there are no Don Juan techniques that will guarantee you a quick lay right away, unless you are after a sleazy chick who will sleep with anyone just because he touched her boobs while drunk.

Do not say anything dumb or insulting to get her attention. A simple hello and just your being yourself is enough to get her attention if she is truly interested.

BE HONEST

Do not start off the relationship with lies. She won't trust you later if you lie from the start.

Comment from an Asian female interviewee:

> *"They should approach me as a person...with mutual respect...and with honesty. Whether you are looking to take me home for the night or to get to know me....let me know...I know a person from the first 5 minutes of talking to them. It is a major turn-off when I have already detected what it is they are looking for, yet they themselves are still beating around the bush....and make me laugh...it's a winner all the time." Jenny, age 29, NY.*

BE VULNERABLE

Many Asian women like guys who are as shy as they are, and who aren't afraid of showing that they are human after all. If you are nervous in approaching an Asian lady, then tell her straight out that you are nervous instead of trying to cover it up by being obnoxious or macho. Remember, most women love guys who are humble and not full of themselves.

BE INTELLIGENT AND BEHAVE

A man should approach a woman with either an intellectually stimulating conversation or a witty comment that is not too personal. Asian women don't like men who ask stupid questions or make comments containing sexual innuendos.

Approach as Many Women as Possible

One reader told me that he approaches four women a day, and that by the end of the month he would have at least one girlfriend. This is a great idea! Try to approach four women a day on the street, on the train, in restaurants, in clubs, and on the Internet dating sites. Give them your business card or ask for their numbers. You are virtually guaranteed a few calls from some of the women you hand your card to or approach. Remember, some women are shy; more often than not, they welcome your interest. And if the woman you approach is not available, perhaps she has a friend who is. Hey, you never know! Your goal is to give your name and number to as many women as possible and to see where that takes you. Just be sure not to appear a "player," or to let any one woman know of the others. Be brave, be brave, be brave!

Ways to Approach an Asian Woman, as told by my Asian Female Interviewees:

1. *"In a gentlemanly manner."* Yuni, age 29, NY.
2. *"They have to welcome me as a friend first."* Pam, age 24, NY.
3. *"With honesty and romantically, though not pushy."* Jen, age 29, AZ.
4. *"In a non-threatening, open, sweet-smile way."* G.G., age 28, CA.
5. *"Just spit yo best game at me! Be cute."* Delia, age 19, NY.
6. *"Like a person and not like something he wants to f**k (sorry to be so blunt). Just casually say "hi" and strike up a conversation. It's really not that hard. And no cheesy pick- up lines...while it's a good ice-breaker...to get a conversation rolling...it's really retarded."* Pam, WA.
7. *"With some respect... I like guys that are very shy approaching me. I think that's cute!"* Suki, CA.
8. *"In a strong confident manner....very sure of himself (but not cocky)."* Mei Mei, HI.
9. *"A guy should approach me when I'm alone and vice- versa— doing that in front of others is embarrassing for me. He must not

have approached other women before me—if I see that he has, it's a total bust. He shouldn't use some cheesy pick-up line and he shouldn't make comments on my body." Mary, CA.

10. *"They should step-by-step approach, such as give me a phone call, ask me on a date, take me to a romantic dinner or go to the movies; at the first time I meet him I should know his personality and his education."* Betty, NY.
11. *"He should approach me in a nice, well-respected manner, instead of the usual...'Yo gurl, lemme get your number..damn, I want that Asian booty'. He should be confident."* Amy, MA.
12. *"Friendly, open, honest, like a gentleman and with respect."* Nancy, NY.
13. *"In a fun way, no stupid pick-up lines. An honest way."* Tammy, CA.
14. *"He should say hello, introduce himself and say that he is attracted to me and that if I have time, at my convenience, he would like to know me better. He should invite me to a public place, not to his car, and treat me to coffee, tea, snacks, lunch or dinner—whatever is appropriate. He also should not force or coerce me to do anything that is contrary to what I want and be on his best behavior at all times."* Amy, HI.
15. *"The man should act gentle, with respect, and not be pushy."* Victoria, CA.
16. *"Just like you mentioned, race/culture-neutral. We are all individuals and dating is as individual it comes."* May, NY.
17. *"In any way but physically, that's just a pain in the ass. Actually, just don't be a dumbass and all will be well."*
18. *"With respect, honesty and genuine motives."* Candice, MA.
19. *"With respect, not just look at me as a person to hop in bed with."* Betty, NY.
20. *"Every woman has a different standard of what is a good way to be approached, and what is a bad way. Personally, I find that strong come-ons make the guy seem rude and only looking for a quick one-night stand; smooth talkers and cocky men are also a turn-off. A man who is shy in approaching and looks as if he doesn't approach women very often but is taking a special chance with you is what makes me notice."* Sara, CA.

21. *"A man should approach me with respect. I don't like a man who asks stupid questions or makes comments with sexual innuendo."* Rosa, NJ.
22. *"Men, don't use any pick-up lines. Approach the woman directly, be yourself, be cool but don't be suave or you'll come off as a player. Women know you want to sleep with them; don't make it so obvious. Be more interested in her and not what's between her legs."* MeiMei, HI.
23. *"The same way he approaches any other females he is interested in. But no lame lines...and especially none of that "I speak (insert your language here)" or Asian-related topics."* Lisa, NC.
24. *"Ask for directions, just start up a conversation, comment on the weather. If the guy is interesting and attractive to the girl, she will respond if only with a smile."* Laura, MN.
25. *"No lines needed for me, just show sincerity that he is attracted and he is interested in finding more about me as an individual. Tasteful sense of humor is high on my list."* Elle, NY.
26. *"With sincerity and lots of class."* Luna, NY.
27. *"The cutest pick-up line was when a guy asked for a cig and started choking. He said he just wanted to talk to me, and was trying to make an excuse to talk to me."* Evie, NJ.
28. *"Be cute about it...don't try to pull some stupid pick-up line that never works..and that only makes the man look like a fool...and don't try to pull some manly BS...and most importantly...don't go about it trying to act all swift..and slick like most black guys try to do...I like it when a guy acts all cute..and tries to get you to laugh...laughing is a common ground that two can share when you don't know each other...it breaks the ice....then he asks you for your number...i think that's the best way."* Midge, CA.

CHAPTER 12

ELEVEN THINGS YOU SHOULD NEVER SAY TO AN ASIAN WOMAN

We'll do this list the David Letterman way—backwards, so we save the best for last:

In all my years of dating and being encountered by non-Asian men and researching for this book, there are eleven things that I can't stand hearing yet hear so many times over and over again…

11. "Hi! You look like the woman who did my nails."

A reader submitted this one, and I have to say I've never heard this one before. Extremely demeaning.

10. "I would like to show you America."

How do you know she hasn't already seen more of America than you? This is condescending and should be avoided.

Comment from an Asian female interviewee:

> *"Treat me with respect. Don't come up with stupid things about Asian culture. Talk to me about what is going on in this country: politics, newspaper news, weather, etc."* Pam, age 35, WA.

9. "I think Asian women are so sexy."

You are telling her that you think of her as an ASIAN SEX OBJECT. Not a good move.

Comments from Asian female interviewees:

> *"No one wants to be approached for their ethnicity. Just as they would probably not like it if I came up and said, "I love white boys, I knew a white boy once who spoke English, maybe you know him?"" S.J., age 26, NY.*

> *"A lot of pick-up lines I get are directed towards my ethnicity and it is those men I chose to ignore. All minorities in this country are sensitive to remarks about their ethnicity from other ethnic groups. Making a comment about ethnicity is a sure way to get a women's guard up." May, age 30, NJ.*

8. "I like you Orientals."

Asians are people; Orientals are rugs. Also, you are not making her feel special if you are grouping her with all the other "Orientals." Remember, a woman wants to feel like she's the only one you're interested in.

7. "What's your accent?" or "Where are you from?"

You are telling her you think of her as different, and most Asians would rather be treated like the Americans they are as they are born, raised, and are living in the United States.

6. "*Ni hao ma?*" ("How are you?" in Mandarin Chinese)

How do you know she's Chinese? This might be good if she were Chinese, but if she's not you risk offending her. Save your language skills for later, when you get to know her better.

Comment from an Asian female interviewee:

> "Men shouldn't greet an Asian woman with the only foreign greeting they know. Most likely, the woman doesn't understand it because it is the right language but wrong woman. I feel offended sometimes, because they greet me with Japanese or Korean, which is rude. I am Chinese, and it'd be nice if they would find out where I am from first before they show off with the only foreign greeting they know." Ling, 29, IL.

5. "Hey, I'm bigger and better than an Asian man."

Do not insult anyone. It will just make you look bad.

Comment from an Asian female interviewee:

> "He should not talk trash about Asian men as a way of picking me up. And also "chink" or "chinky" should not be used AT ANY GIVEN TIME." Sally, 29, NY.

4. "Is it true that Asian women are wild in bed?" or "Why are Asian women so kinky?" or anything of that nature.

Would you want someone to say these things to your mother or sister? If not, don't say them at all.

Comment from an Asian female interviewee:

> "Anything that starts with, "You all Asian women...." or..."I heard you Asian girls...." UGH....I HATE HATE HATE THAT....it's generalizing a whole bunch of us into this one stereotype! "Can you tie a cherry stem into a knot with your tongue...I heard all Asian women can do it....you have that special mouth thing." THIS LINE....first made me laugh..then I took his cherry stem.. tied it

into a knot, and told him if he wanted me to make animal balloons as well, all he need do was ask. One guy said..."I heard Asian women are kinky and great in bed." WHATEVER....pick-up lines do not make me feel degraded...I take them as an open opportunity to let them know how dumb and closed-minded they sound. I don't belittle them...I just basically try to let them know how much more there is to know about this specific "Asian" girl they happen to approach." H.J., age 21, NY.

3. "Are you Korean or Japanese?" or anything of a similar nature.

This is a question you should not ask immediately after you meet an Asian woman.

2. Anything dealing with kimonos, slanted body parts, chopsticks, geishas, China dolls, etc.

She does not want you to stereotype her. She is a person.

AND FINALLY, MY PERSONAL FAVORITE:

1. "Do you speak English?"

If you say this to anyone, HELLO? Where were you raised, in a cave? See the chapter in this book entitled "How to Approach an Asian Lady" for further discussion on this topic.

CHAPTER 13

HOW TO ACT ON A FIRST DATE WITH AN ASIAN WOMAN

You must be on your best behavior on the first date. Some pointers:

- Do not talk about your ex-girlfriends, especially Asian ex-girlfriends if you are a non-Asian guy
- If you are an Asian guy, don't talk about your white ex-girlfriends. Asian girls generally think that Asian guys who bring up their white ex-girlfriends in conversation are bragging. Just don't talk about ex-girlfriends!
- Do not smoke
- Be yourself
- Do not concentrate too much on her Asian ethnicity
- Do not call Asians by the term "Orientals"
- Do not put down Asian men
- Do not talk about sex
- Pay attention to her, and do not look around the room for other women
- Pay for the date and do not talk about money
- Be fun, relaxed, and happy

Nowadays, men are more and more confused about dating etiquette. Should he open the doors, or wait for the lady to exit the elevator first? Some men are so puzzled by what to do in certain social situations that they instead become awkward and thus risk the chance of having the lady think he doesn't have any manners at all. Unless your date has told you that she is an ultra-modern woman who is extremely independent and believes in equality between men and women, 50/50 all the way, assume that she would like to be treated like a lady, the old-fashioned way. This means that you are to wait for her to get out of an elevator first (I cannot believe how many men do not follow this important rule of etiquette!), hold doors open for her, pay for dinner and behave like a gentleman.

You must arrive on time. Lots of Asian ladies have reported getting turned off after a guy shows up late for a date. You do not want to spoil your chances of dating an Asian lady by being late, so always give yourself plenty of time for travel. Better to arrive early than to make your Asian woman wait!

If you are meeting your date in person for the first time after emailing or chatting over the Internet, then she probably does not want you to know where she lives until she gets to knows you better. In such cases, you should offer to pick her up at work or at home, while expecting her to say that she will meet you in a public place. Understand that this might be for her own safety and not because she doesn't like you.

If you met through friends or have known each other for some time in other situations, she would probably expect you to pick her up at her home or office—even if you do not have a car. This is something guys in metropolitan areas such as New York City have to watch out for, since many guys in New York don't own automobiles. Picking up your date just makes her feel more special. If a man is doing the driving, he should open the door for the lady when they get to the car and also when they arrive at their destination. It may seem awkward to you at first, but you will be thought of as a gentleman. Remember, respect is very important in Asian cultures. WARNING: For Americanized Asian-Americans, too much of this might seem patronizing or too cavalier.

During the date, remember that she is just as nervous as you are. So relax and concentrate on being yourself and on having a good time. Don't worry about whether she likes you or not because she is probably wondering the same thing about you. A nice, polite compliment at the beginning of the date with a smile would make her warm up to you. You can compliment her on her outfit or on how wonderful she looks. Just be sure not to use any sexually suggestive compliments. For example, say:

"You look lovely tonight."
"You look even more beautiful than you do in your photo."

And DO NOT say:

"Gosh, all you Orientals are so gorgeous."
"I love you sexy Asian women."
"That dress shows off your beautiful behind."

Take her to a nice place; it does not matter whether it is expensive or not so long as it's nice. What do I mean by "nice" and how do you figure out what's "nice" and what's not for your first date with your Asian lady? Talk to your Asian lady before the date and make your decision on where to go from your conversation. I remember being very impressed by a gentleman who decided that we would go hiking and have a picnic after having a conversation with me during which I mentioned the fact that I like the outdoors. In my experience, the most popular Asian cuisine among Asians is Japanese, so perhaps your date would like to go for some Japanese food. There are always restaurant ads in the Chinese newspapers, each touting the sushi selection in the advertised restaurant's buffets in order to attract more customers. Keep in mind that some Asian women might be shy and therefore prefer not to eat in front of strangers. If you have this suspicion, ask your Asian date if she would like to have dinner or just coffee. Or you can just decide to meet for coffee or tea, and then go to dinner if you two hit it off over a few cups at a nice café.

Many Asians have alcohol dehydrogenase deficiency, which means that they lack the enzyme used to digest alcohol. According to *The Merck Manual*, 50% of Chinese and Japanese and other people of

Asian descent lack aldehyde dehydrogenase-2, an enzyme involved in ethanol metabolism. This might result in alcohol intolerance, flushing of the face, muscle weakness, nausea, and other nasty symptoms whenever any alcohol is ingested. I am not a doctor, but I know from personal experience that I get really nauseous and weak when I ingest even a small amount of alcohol. I find it cumbersome to have to explain my alcohol intolerance to people who don't understand that this affects a large percentage of the Asian population. People make me feel like it's antisocial not to drink; little do they know it's actually physical! So now that you know this, you can impress your Asian date with your understanding of Asians and alcohol dehydrogenase deficiency. You will get extra points here because most people, except for doctors, do not know about this.

Depending on the lady, she might prefer to eat Asian food, especially if she has just arrived from Asia. Ask her what she prefers to eat to make sure that she will be happy with the food. Many Asians do not like cheese or milk products due to their unfamiliarity with milk and dairy intolerance (my mother gags at the thought of cheese and doesn't eat ice cream despite having lived in the United States for over twenty years). Studies show that around 90% of Asians are lactose intolerant. Aversion to dairy products is less strong for Asians raised in the United States. One exception seems to be ice cream, which is selling well in Asian markets. Asian countries are increasingly demanding exported dairy products due to the Westernization of Asian diets, so perhaps your Asian friend is used to consuming dairy products.

Some Asians take their tea very seriously and do not like the American variety, so you might impress your Asian lady by learning a bit about tea (one source you can check out is www.TenRen.com). During the date, she might not eat too much, since some Asian women are very self-conscious about their weight (I've seen lots of diet pills sold in Asian beauty salons) and she might not feel too comfortable eating in front of strangers. Also, concentrate on the ambiance, not the food, and on whether you two can talk and get to know each other better.

How to Act on a First Date

You should be a gentleman and pay for the first date. Many Asian women have reported to me that they are accustomed to excellent treatment by their dates. Do not be cheap and insist on equality here or you might not see her again. This is one area where I insist on not being "politically correct"—you bought this book in order to learn about the things that impress an Asian woman from the point of view of an Asian woman herself; trust my advice. Sure, there might be a minority of people who disagree with me, but do yourself a favor and pay for the first date.

On a date, you may show interest in Asian culture (do not mention Asian culture immediately upon meeting an Asian woman); however, do not be condescending about it. Refer to Asians as Asians and never refer to people as "Orientals." It is cute to say a few words of whatever language the lady happens to speak, since by now she would probably have told you where she is from and what languages she speaks. This will probably not apply to Americanized Asian-Americans, who often do not speak any Asian languages.

Do not talk too much about yourself. Focus your attention on her. This will make her feel special and give you clues on where to take her for your next date.

If you think you would like to see her again, then ask her questions regarding what she would like to do on subsequent dates. I'd suggest talking in general about museums or music, and then see what she says. If she says she loves Rodin, then you can be sure that she would like it if you asked her to go see the Rodin exhibit or something related at a museum on your next date.

As a man, you should always hold open the doors and wait for your lady to walk into a room before you. Again, you might think that this is over-doing it by Western standards, but in her eyes doing such things makes you a true gentleman.

At the end of the date, you should bring the lady safely to her home, or at least wait until the lady gets into a cab. If she doesn't know you very well, she may not want you to know where she lives.

This is particularly true if you just had your first date after meeting on the Internet.

The following applies if she does indeed know you well enough to trust you: If you want to be romantic then you need to do some extra work and spend the extra time and money to take the taxi with her back home (or driving her home), even if you think it's not likely that she'll ask you to spend the night. Walking the lady to her door would also get you on her good side. I speak both from experience and from my research. If you need examples, see the dating etiquette section of Http://www.Cupidsworld.com, where an Asian lady complains about a date who didn't wait for the bus with her.

Be a gentleman during the entire evening, including at the end of the night. Do not try to push her too early into kissing or other physical activities. Try to read her by her actions toward you to determine whether she likes you enough to want to kiss you. If the girl shows signs of being attracted to you such as touching you, holding your hand, smiling, laughing, and so on, then it is safe to kiss her. Otherwise, a hug would do nicely. Also, keep in mind that it is often taboo in Asian culture to kiss in public; your Asian date might be reluctant to show any public displays of affection even if she likes you. See, for example, Virtualtourist.com (this site says that public displays of affection not welcomed in Asian cultures) and http://www.worldinformation.com/World/Asia/Japan/guide.asp?country=081 (this site says that kissing in public is impolite in Japan). Always err on the side of being conservative and respectful. Your Asian lady would appreciate the respect you have shown her and be more receptive to your affection later on. Most of the Asian ladies I interviewed mentioned that the worst thing a man can do on a first date is to make an unwanted sexual advance.

CHAPTER 14

WHAT TO DO TO GET AN ASIAN WOMAN TO GO OUT WITH YOU AGAIN

How do you get a great Asian woman to go out with you again?

The most important thing is that you assume that she liked you and call the lady the next day, unless the date went really badly. I have heard too many stories about how the guy thought the Asian lady did not like him when actually she was just too shy to show it or was just waiting for the guy to call. When in doubt, always call within 24 hours of the date. You don't have anything to lose. There is really nothing to getting her to go out with you again, just ask! I surveyed lots of Asian ladies and most of them said that they expect the guy to call them the next day if their first date went well.

How many times should you keep on asking her out for the second and subsequent dates? Take your cue from her response to you. If she seems genuinely enthusiastic about another date, but seems busy for the moment, then definitely keep in touch. However, if she does not return any of your phone calls or emails or seems elusive about another date then you should probably not push the issue. The worse thing you can do is to call too often and leave desperate messages on her machine when she doesn't seem interested. Pay attention to what she says and does in order to tell if she is interested in another date.

It is a nice touch to send some flowers (just don't send white or yellow chrysanthemums, as they are for funerals in many Asian cultures). Two elegant suggestions are plum and cherry blossoms, which are popular with Asians. Both look like small branches of a tree with little buds of flowers. The plum blossom, the national flower of Taiwan (Republic of China), symbolizes purity, elegance and intelligence. In 1912, Japan presented the United States with over 3,000 cherry blossom trees as a gift of friendship. These cherry blossom trees were planted in Washington, D.C., the site of the National Cherry Blossom Festival every year. Just the other day, I went to Dean & Deluca in Soho in New York (a great place for exotic flowers) and bought a huge branch of cherry blossoms. I walked over to Pottery Barn to get a vase for my cherry blossoms and at least five people, including two Asian women, came up to me to compliment me on my flowers. These blossoms were so unusual-looking that people felt compelled to talk to me about them. Here's an idea for you gentlemen. Why don't you buy some unusual-looking flowers like cherry blossoms and walk around the street with them? Some people suggest that one walk one's dog as a way to meet women, so why not walk around with flowers? Dogs are too common nowadays anyway. And, if you meet a very special woman while carrying the flowers, why don't you give them to her? That would definitely make her notice you.

Very few guys send flowers anymore, so you will definitely stand out in her mind and in her heart if you did such a thing. It is almost every woman's dream to get a bouquet of flowers sent to the office after a great date! You might even want to send it to the office so she can show the flowers off to her co-workers. This makes you look good because it shows that you are thoughtful.

Also, it's a good idea to suggest another date based on what she has said to you on your previous date. Many Asians like karaoke, so perhaps that is a good idea for another date. Again, it really depends on the lady; if you did your research by asking her what her likes and dislikes are during your first date, you would have the advantage of already knowing her preferences for subsequent dates. Do your research!

How to Get a Second Date

Also, watch that you do not wear the same outfits over and over again in your ensuing dates. Some Asian ladies have complained that a few men they've dated kept on wearing the same clothes. You want to appear neat and professional, so dress accordingly.

Something to keep in mind, and that sadly will apply no matter how many dates you go on with your Asian girlfriend: If you are a non-Asian dating an Asian woman, keep in mind that there will probably be certain prejudiced individuals who will make upsetting comments about your relationship. These people are either jealous, narrow-minded, or both. You must defend your Asian woman's pride and tell these people off if they say anything stupid in front of her. Do not ever take the side of these prejudiced individuals, no matter how close you are to them. This is especially hard if these people are related to you; however, you must take your Asian girlfriend's side in such situations or you will see her disappear really fast. Concentrate on the beauty of your relationship and standing up for your woman. Ignore the negative comments. Your relationship with your girlfriend is a matter that goes beyond her race or yours, and therefore a matter that you should defend whenever it's being disparaged by other people. They are probably just jealous of your happiness.

CHAPTER 15

WHAT MAKES A MAN SEXY?

No, guys, you do not have to be bodybuilder or a *GQ* model to be desirable. In fact, most Asian women I interviewed simply wanted men who were approachable and clean- looking. All of the things that I suggest to make yourself sexy are very doable and not hard at all; any man can do these things to make himself more appealing to women. The following is a list of what makes a man sexy, according to the Asian women I interviewed:

1. Good Grooming

The Asian ladies who I interviewed said that the most important factor in sexiness in a man is cleanliness. Women get turned off very easily when a guy smells bad or has perspiration problems or bad odors. Therefore, it is very important that you groom yourself very well to avoid offending the woman of your dreams.

2. An Attractive Appearance with a Great Body

You do not have to be a model, but you should take care of yourself and care about your appearance. Sure, there are some things that you cannot help, such as a receding hairline or your height. However, there are lots of things you can do to make yourself even more attractive:

Get a good haircut
Eat healthy
Exercise
Get adequate sleep
Dress neatly

3. Self-Confidence

Many women find it sexy when you are self-confident and can approach them in a confident manner. However, do not act arrogant, as this can turn Asian women off. In my opinion, arrogance is when a man brags too much about his power and possessions. This also signifies that the man is insecure. A confident man will approach a woman even though he fears rejection.

4. Intelligence

A man's mind is often his sexiest part, especially to an Asian woman. Education is highly valued in Asian societies, and part of being intelligent is often education. Also, intelligence allows you to carry on great conversations, which is very, very sexy.

5. Romance

Women find it very sexy when a man buys or does nice things for her just because. Therefore, you should buy flowers, give her kisses, take her to nice places, remember anniversaries and her birthday, and shower her with affection just because you love her.

6. Masculinity

Women find masculine men very attractive. We Asian women want to be the ones who are feminine, so act strong and manly.

7. Shyness and Vulnerability

A lot of women find shy and vulnerable men very sexy, because it shows that the man is a person. Even if you are tough on the outside, revealing a bit of vulnerability warms a woman's heart.

8. Honesty

No one wants to be with a liar. Do not pretend to be someone you are not. Be honest in every way possible.

9. Loyalty

Many Asian ladies told me that Asian women require more loyalty than other ladies. Be faithful!

10. Ambition

Your will to succeed in business and life will excite her. Many women prefer hard-working professionals.

11. Sense of Humor

A woman wants a man who can make her laugh and not take things so seriously.

My Asian female interviewees tell you what they find sexy in a man:

> *"Loyalty, charm, passion, wit, danger, excitement, mystery, masculinity ..." Lisa, CA.*

> *"The way they treat you, the way they show you how much they care and the way they look at you as if you are the most beautiful thing they've ever seen." Mary, NJ.*

> *"His personality always makes him sexy. A man who can make me laugh and who loves kids will do that too. It's a man's sensitive side that is very attractive." C.M., TX.*

"Eyes and height and sense of romance." Mary, TX.

"Being gentle and caring about a woman's mind...But at least men have to care about how they look like and what to wear, too." Jen, MA.

"The smell of cologne which I like." B.J., AZ.

"His physical appearance (I'm sorry, I'm really big on this one), his mannerisms, his manners, his charm, his wit, his intelligence, his sense of humor, his friendliness, his openness." Kerry, NY.

"Personality, smile, eyes..." Kim, NJ.

"A man is sexy when he is kind and shows true interest in the person. Asks about what she likes, does not say he knows how to use chopsticks or any other random Asian trivia." Maria, CA.

"Confident but not egotistical. Good conversation skills, positive and humorous personality. Sexy is mainly in the attitude." T.M., NY.

"The way he presents himself....classy...stylish...the way he moves....the way he talks....the way he makes you feel when he looks at you...that's sexy." May, CA.

"If he is self-assured without being cocky. Not cheap, but not in your face about his wealth. Dresses decent, neat...not wrinkled and sweaty. A man with a sense of humor is very sexy." Nancy, NY.

"The way a man carries and presents himself is what makes him sexy. Having a great personality is a plus." E.L., CA.

"His personality by far....his body language." Kelly, HI.

"Athletic body, good fashion, good height, good at sex." Tania, NJ.

"Their smiles, the look in their eyes... The way they can make you giggle or something girly like that. Anything can make one sexy, as long as one knows how to use it." Lisa, CA.

"His beautiful, sincere smile and genuine interest in me as a person. He also has bedroom eyes and we connect electrically." Jasmine, IL.

"I think a man's intelligence makes him sexy. I love quick wit and cockiness." Barbara, MA.

Bibliography/ Recommended Reading

A Profile of the Nation's Foreign-Born Population from Asia (2000 Update), Issued February 2002, United States Census Bureau. (Go to Census.gov.)

Chinese American History Timeline, http://www.itp.berkeley.edu/~asam121/timeline.html

Chinese Culture Center, http://www.c-c-c.org

Fletcher, Michael A., Interracial Marriages Eroding Barriers, *Washington Post*, December 28, 1998, http://www.washingtonpost.com/wp-srv/national/daily/dec98/melt29.htm.

Population Change and Distribution, Census 2000 Brief, 1990 to 2000, Issued April 2001, United States Census Bureau.

Spooner, Tom, Asian-Americans and the Internet: The young and connected, Pew Internet & American Life Project, December 12, 2001, http://www.pewinternet.org

The Asian Population 2000, Census 2000 Brief, Issued February 2002, United States Census Bureau.

The University of Michigan, Intimate Relationships between Races More Common Than Thought, March 23, 2000, http://www.umich.edu/~newsinfo/Releases/2000/Mar00/r032300a.html

Tomoyuki, Tanaka, Disparity in Asian/White Interracial Dating FAQ, 1995, http://www.cs.indiana.edu/hyplan/tanaka/disparity/disparity.txt.

Sucheng Chan, *Asian Americans: An Interpretive History* (Gale, 1991).
This book covers all the issues and most of the important aspects of and events in Asian-American history.

Departing Words

I hope this book has been helpful. The most important things to keep in mind in order to have successful relationships with Asian women are to treat them with respect and to understand Asian culture.

Remember, you will never get the girl if you don't ask her out, so be brave, be brave, be brave! I KNOW that summoning up the courage to approach a woman can sometimes be the hardest thing to do, but you must take risks if you want to have the woman of your dreams. Remember, armed with the information in this book you are way ahead of all the other men out there trying to pursue an Asian girlfriend. Have confidence in yourself, remember the things I've said, and just approach her!

You are invited to join the Asian American Professionals Network at http://www.AsianSocials.com. This is a network for professionals interested in socializing and networking with other professionals in the U.S. and all over the world.

If you have any questions or comments, please email me at Ming@AsianSocials.com

Thank you.

Ming Tan
Ming@AsianSocials.com
New York City, USA

Printed in the United States
69281LVS00007B/247